System Leadership in Practice

System Leadership in Practice

*Rob Higham, David Hopkins
and Peter Matthews*

Open University Press

Open University Press
McGraw-Hill Education
McGraw-Hill House
Shoppenhangers Road
Maidenhead
Berkshire
England
SL6 2QL

email: enquiries@openup.co.uk
world wide web: www.openup.co.uk

and Two Penn Plaza, New York, NY 10121-2289, USA

First published 2009

A catalogue record of this book is available from the British Library

ISBN-13: 978 033 5236114 (pb) 978 033 5236121 (hb)
ISBN-10: 033 5236111 (pb) 033 523612X (hb)

Library of Congress Cataloging-in-Publication Data
CIP data applied for

Typeset by YHT Ltd, London
Printed in the UK by Bell and Bain Ltd, Glasgow

Fictitious names of companies, products, people, characters and/or data that may be used herein (in case studies or in examples) are not intended to represent any real individual, company, product or event.

Mixed Sources
Product group from well-managed forests and other controlled sources
www.fsc.org   Cert no. TT-COC-002769
© 1996 Forest Stewardship Council

The **McGraw·Hill** *Companies*

To our parents

The three of us are very mindful that whatever we have achieved in our lives we owe to our parents. We are also keenly aware that they are all passing through important transitions in their own lives. We therefore dedicate this book to them:

From Rob to Jo and John

From David to Cliff and Thelma

From Peter to B. and John

With thanks for their love and support.

Contents

Preface		ix
Acknowledgements		xi
Acronyms and abbreviations		xii
1	Power to the professionals: the emergence of system leadership	1
2	Mapping the system leadership landscape	18
3	Leadership of sustained improvement in challenging contexts	31
4	Leading innovation and improvement partnerships: the case of Leading Edge	51
5	Leadership in the context of Every Child Matters: extended, full service and community schools	72
6	Executive leadership and federations	91
7	Change agents of school transformation: consultant leaders, National Leaders of Education and their schools	107
8	The prospects for system leadership	128
	Notes	147
	References	151
	Index	159

Preface

We have become increasingly intrigued over the past decade with the concept of system leadership. From our various positions in government, universities and Ofsted, and also in having a penchant for practice, we began to see a shift in culture and attitude among the school leaders we were engaging with. There was, increasingly, a dramatic shift in attitude and practice from the voracious competition of the mid-1990s to a more benign attitude to collaboration. Partially stimulated by policy initiatives such as Education Action Zones and Excellence in Cities, system leadership was also apparent in the local collaborations to improve student learning in which many headteachers and other leaders were involved. We began to realize that this was not just a passing fad or some comfortable but essentially simplistic approach to networking. It was instead a potentially radical shift in the landscape of education. The ubiquity of top-down change and prescription was being replaced by more authentic forms of collaborative and lateral activity and focused increasingly on enhancing student learning. In some cases, this was leading to alternative forms of governance and structural arrangements, stimulated in part by the National College for School Leadership and, as it then was, the Specialist Schools Trust. We began to realize that we may be witnessing the emergence of a movement that had the potential to transform the English educational system.

In our various ways, particularly when, in the mid-2000s, we were all in some way in government, we did what we could to support this movement through trying to help make a shift from an educational system that was, essentially, characterized by national prescription to one that was increasingly led by schools. Having left government, we all found ourselves, a few years ago, associated with the London Centre for Leadership in Learning at the Institute of Education, University of London. Increasingly, we began to focus our research and development energy on the phenomenon of 'system leadership' in its various guises. This led, inevitably, to increasing collaborative work and the commitment to write this book.

In preparing the book, we were determined to make this a collaborative effort. So, although we have taken individual responsibility for different chapters – hence some differences in style – our combined work on each of them has improved the original markedly. We were also conscious that we were writing at a time that was volatile in terms of policy and practice: so much so that events have inevitably moved on in some respects during the course of publication. For example, the National Challenge, with all its implications for system leadership, was announced as we were in the final stages of preparing the manuscript. We have included reference to the National Challenge in the text, but waiting longer to write and publish we felt would be futile. We say this because we are confident that we have identified trends and practices that have a medium- and even long-term relevance for practice, policy and research.

Rob Higham, David Hopkins and Peter Matthews
London Centre for Leadership in Learning, September 2008

Acknowledgements

We have incurred many debts along the way. The first debt of gratitude is to the new breed of system leaders who have inspired us. They include, among many others: Alan Roach, Sir Alan Steer, Barry Day, Bushra Nasir, David Dunckley, David Hawker, Sir Dexter Hutt, George Berwick, Graeme Hollinshead, Jack Harrison, Sir Kevin Satchwell, Michael Wilkins, Mick Meadows, Paul Grant, Sue Glanville, Susan John and Terry Fish.

The second is to the policy makers and policy influencers from whom we have learned so much. In government we would like to identify, in particular, the contribution and support from Estelle Morris and David Miliband; from national agencies, Elizabeth Reid, David Crossley and Sue Williamson (Specialist Schools and Academies Trust), Steve Munby, Colin Connor, Toby Salt and Di Barnes (the National College for School Leadership); and others whose support and advice have been critical: Dame Mary Richardson, Tom Bentley, Tony Mackay, Tim Brighouse, Michael Fullan, Pam Sammons and Robert Hill.

Third, we thank those great colleagues and friends who have worked alongside us over the past three years and have contributed to what appears on the following pages; thanks to Elpida Ahtaridou, Karen Edge, Jan Robertson and Jenny Andreae. We are very grateful to Janet Brennan who did a brilliant job of proof-reading the manuscript and saved us from much embarrassment!

Fourth, we acknowledge the support we have had from a number of organizations that have funded our research. Thanks to the Research Councils UK, the Specialist Schools and Academies Trust, the National College for School Leadership, HSBC Education Trust, the Organisation for Economic Co-operation and Development and Commonwealth Research.

Finally, in dedicating this book to our parents we also thank our families for their support. Particular thanks to Alpa for all her love and encouragement.

We hope that all those we have acknowledged will see the part they played in what follows and realize what a contribution they are making to ensuring that we really do achieve an educational system where every person is able to fulfil their potential.

Acronyms and abbreviations

APA   Annual Performance Assessment
CPD   continuing professional development
CVA   contextually value-added (score)
CYPT   Children and Young People's Trust
DCSF   Department for Children, School and Families
DfES   Department for Education and Skills
ECM   Every Child Matters
FSES   full-service extended school
FSM   free school meals
lCT   information and communication technology
LEPP   Leading Edge Partnership Programme
LLS   London Leadership Strategy
LMS   local management of schools
NCSL   National College for School Leadership
NLE   National Leader of Education
NPQH   National Professional Qualification for Headship
NSS   National Support School
OECD   Organisation for Economic Co-operation and Development
Ofsted   Office for Standards in Education, Children's Services and Skills
SIP   school improvement partner
SMT   senior management team
SSAT   Specialist Schools and Academies Trust
VLE   virtual learning environment

1 Power to the professionals: the emergence of system leadership

Ask schools about the purpose of education and almost all will talk about fulfilling each student's potential. Ask how and most will set out a vision of a healthy mix of knowledge, skills and qualifications, the well-being of every child and their preparation for adult life. National education systems, however, have often failed to harness the combined capacity of their many thousands of schools to advance this vision in practice. In England, there are about 23,000 state schools, 450,000 teachers and senior leaders and 300,000 support staff. What they do on a daily basis has an impact directly on the life chances of about 7.5 million young people. Yet, in discharging this enormous responsibility, schools have traditionally remained relatively independent or even purposefully disconnected from one another. While there are exceptions, pedagogy that might have been effective in individual schools has not been easily shared or validated at a wider level. Too few schools have reached beyond their own capacity to collaboratively develop exciting provision or support one another in difficult times. As a result, the wheels of education appear to have been reinvented many times over. In this book, we argue that a solution to this state of affairs appears to be emerging. This, we suggest, results from a new set of national policies, professional practices and, in particular, the work of school leaders who act as system leaders.

There are many reasons for the historical isolation of schools. While teaching inherently demands social interaction, its practice usually remained behind the classroom door or the school gate. The consequences of state policy have often been to keep it so. A potted English history provides some evidence. In the post-war 1940s, the priority was to develop a coherent state education system out of disparate local provision. The blueprint was for a 'national system, locally administered' with schools connected more by policy circulars than by any planned interaction.[1] By the 1970s, more widespread professional innovation had emerged. Yet, despite notable exceptions and the work of some local authorities, schools often remained unconnected and it remained hard to share with the many the really innovative advances of the few. In the 1980s, Thatcherism brought market forces into the public sector to act as a spur to improvement. Schools were given delegated budgets. They were empowered to make decisions about resources but became increasingly embroiled in competitive relations, particularly with open enrolment, regular inspection reports and the publication of national test and examination results. Some cooperation survived, and even prospered, but this was marginalized for many years at a national level. Subsequent efforts to spread good practice from the centre were too often undermined by a prescriptive approach and limits to local ownership by schools.

Two-thirds of a century on from the initial post-war blueprint, there is evidence of a widespread and unprecedented drawing together of schools. The impetus, we argue, lies in a new alignment of specific government policies, the work of some local authorities and, ultimately, the leadership of schools themselves. From about the turn of the millennium, moves were made in government towards a sponsoring of school collaboration, in part as a response to the excesses of market reforms. A number of national agencies and local authorities followed suit by facilitating networks among schools and engaging them in network design. Many school leaders have taken up these opportunities and/or aligned them to existing local partnerships. What is proving decisive is the emergence of a new type of school leader that we are calling a system leader. Put simply, a system leader is a headteacher or senior teacher who works directly for the success and well-being of students in other schools as well as his or her own.

Such system leadership is relatively new. It goes substantial beyond the collaborative activities in which schools in England are increasingly engaged. There are, however, many leadership teams contemplating the challenge of taking on strategic roles beyond their own school. This book argues that a small but growing number of system leaders are a powerful force for change and improvement. These are leaders who innovate, take risks and deploy resources creatively. They have a deep understanding of pedagogy and how it can be improved. They see collaboration with other schools as vital to deliver on aims that individual schools simply cannot achieve alone. Above all, they are leaders of schools that are willing and able to work for improvement in the wider system.

In this book we focus purposefully on school-led *system leadership in practice*. We do so in the light of new research evidence which begins to illuminate the methods and impact of system leaders. We encounter such leaders in local authorities and national agencies but our focus is on the school and inter-school levels. We explore how and why such system leadership is developing, its practices and outcomes as well as potential future trends and policy implications. We identify and interrogate in detail five key system leadership roles. These are:

- leadership that sustains improvements in very challenging contexts and then shares its experience, knowledge and practice with other schools;

- leadership of collaborative innovations in curriculum and pedagogy;
- leadership that brokers and shapes radically new networks of extended services and student welfare across local communities;
- leadership of improvement across a formal partnership of schools;
- leadership that acts as an external agent of change in other schools that face significant difficulties.

We believe that undertaking these roles, and mobilizing school and system resources to do so, represents perhaps the most demanding yet profound educational leadership challenge of our times. In short, we see system leaders to offer a vision of how professionals working together can lead educational renewal and the impact it can have on society.

Talk of a new era of professionalism may sound highly idealistic, especially at a time when, for many people, government tests and accountability constrain the purpose of education. It will also be contested, as some see system leaders only as functionaries of the state who coordinate local toil towards nationally defined targets. Yet, despite these criticisms, the progressive potential of system leadership has excited real interest among many stakeholders in education. It is seen to offer alternative solutions to educational challenges that have traditionally remained the preserve of the central state. It is also seen to have implications for wider debates about centralism, localism and the optimal distribution of decision-making power in public services.

In this initial chapter, we begin to explore these perspectives by providing a short recent history of school-to-school collaboration. We then locate our argument in the wider concerns for top-down versus bottom-up reform before developing the notion of a new professionalism. This leads to our focus on the emergence of system leadership before we finally summarize the purpose and structure of the book.

A recent history of school collaboration

It is estimated that nearly all schools in England are now involved in some form of networking (Hill 2006). This state of affairs would have been hard to anticipate during the late 1990s. A New Labour government came to power in England in 1997 having coined the now famous slogan 'Education, Education, Education'. The promise was for educational renewal and a healthy dose of 'progressive universalism' aimed at improving school standards and social equity simultaneously. In reality, at the systemic level, New Labour's main approach was to evolve the more radical reforms introduced in the 1980s under Margaret Thatcher, albeit in a context of significantly higher public spending. Thatcher's Conservatives had introduced an educational market to unleash competition-driven improvements. New Labour sought to advance market effectiveness through greater parental choice coupled with the diversification of schools away from a common comprehensive model and towards institutional differentiation by curriculum specialisms. Similarly, where the Conservatives had introduced the National Curriculum and national tests, New Labour developed accompanying National Strategies that summarized a range of effective pedagogic approaches and promoted a minimum set that schools and teachers were strongly encouraged to implement.

It was at the more specific level of schools facing challenging circumstances that New Labour initially unleashed a range of funded initiatives aimed at school collaboration for excellence and equity. The Excellence in Cities programme, for instance, sought to share capacity for teaching, learning and community engagement across urban schools. The Leadership Incentive Grant aimed to strengthen leadership in schools through collaborative professional development and mentoring. A growing number of specialist schools were expected to work with other schools to spread good practice and raise standards. The list of initiatives went on. It might have appeared contradictory to the broader approach of market-led competition. But this was New Labour and its 'Third Way' philosophy that prioritized eclectic pragmatism over ideological chastity. Thus, on the one hand, the forces of market competition, external (consumer) standards and government regulation were combined with, on the other hand, collaboration, the sharing of best practice and the increasing professional status of school leaders.

By 2003, the government felt sufficiently confident to argue that there were now 'system-wide benefits' to schools working in partnership (DfES 2003: 12). A range of reasons exist for this. Several hold clues to our later discussion of system leadership. First, faced with the limits of 'command and control' policies, as well as the system inequalities that can result from competition, networks held the appeal of greater professional engagement, lateral working and system coherence (Glatter 2003). Second, there was an existing need for joint working in practice to resolve interconnected challenges in, for example, student welfare (Osbourne 2000). Sharing of power between institutions was thus partly driven by legislation but also by 'organisations coming together voluntarily, either to exploit opportunities for additional resources or to resolve perceived problems' (Connolly and James 2006: 69). Third, this was to some extent a rediscovery of the professional collaborations that had been facilitated by local education authorities in around the 1970s and 1980s (Glatter 1995; Stevenson 2007). But now central initiatives were combining with the agency of educators, for whom the impulse to collaborate had 'never died; instead, it had persisted, but had become more difficult to express' (Hannon 2007: 135).

A decade or so on from 1997, we now have a growing sense of the potential benefits of collaboration between schools as well as with other agencies and private and voluntary organizations. Of course, different outcomes often relate to local aims, activities and ways of working. However, a range of studies and evaluations have found a relatively high degree of similarity in the benefits that can be achieved where partnerships are effective. These are summarized in Table 1.1.

Table 1.1   Commonly quoted benefits of collaboration[2]

Good practice:	share effective practice or expertise, identify shared problems and work collaboratively on solutions.
Professional development:	provide mutual and informed support; enhance quality of staff development and critical reflection; joint staffing, wider career structures, solve staffing shortages; improve leadership quality and support and/or whole school systems.
Direct student benefits:	wider curriculum choice and learning pathways; improved transition of pupils into secondary school; raised student expectations and (in some cases) attainment.
Local strategic leadership:	increase equity and reduce polarization of schools; promote coherent provision for local communities; increased community involvement; ensure the survival of rural schools.
Resources:	drawing in additional funding and resources; developing efficiency and economies of scale; reduce risk and uncertainties of innovation and new projects.

Another common message is that achieving these benefits is far from easy, particularly when evidence of an impact on student outcomes is sought. As Vangen and Huxham (2003: 62) found more generally, reports of unmitigated success are not common. Instead, partnerships can develop collaborative inertia in which only hard fought or negligible progress is made. In education, there are a number of obstacles to schools escaping such inertia. At a national level, policy that sponsors collaboration is currently combined with parental choice, competition between schools and the deeply ingrained workings of accountability for individual schools. While similar policy contradictions have a longer history (Levačić and Woods 1994; Aitchison 1995) the current scale of aspiration for collaboration brings these tensions into sharper relief.

At the local level, a variety of circumstances can be found in which contemporary collaboration and competition often coexist in complex muddy waters. At the extreme, there remains 'a spirit of intense competition and mutual suspicion' (Arnold 2006: 6). Some relationships are still framed by 'the pecking order in which they are placed by performance league tables' (Stevenson 2007: 32). There are also the residual scars of policies which allowed some schools to opt out of local authority control. This inevitably has an impact on the ability and desire of schools to overcome other common obstacles to collaboration. These include, as set out in Table 1.2, time, resource constraints and distance. It also becomes more difficult to develop the already demanding practices commonly associated with effective partnerships. These include building trust and the willingness to compromise, surrender some institutional autonomy and bear the costs of partnership work that usually occur before the benefits.

Table 1.2   Commonly quoted factors supporting and obstacles to effective collaboration

Factors supporting effective collaboration

Ethos	Trust, honesty, respect, openness; a sense of joint ownership, with different views taken into account; staff values supporting cooperation; ability to compromise while seeing collaboration in one's interests.
Leadership	Senior leadership commitment; a clearly identified and realist focus that is predominantly shared; monitoring and evaluation of progress.
Activities	A degree of consensus on the methods that will lead to success; purpose directly connected with needs of specific learners; a focus on goals that individual partners could not achieve alone.

Obstacles to effective collaboration

Resources	time/distance; lack of funding; costs often occurring before benefits.
Leadership	apprehension of staff not acknowledged; poor communication; silo mentality; unwillingness to negotiate sovereignty.
History	a culture of competition; difficulty of working across old structures.

What is significant, in many places, is that obstacles to collaboration are being surmounted and a new interconnectedness developed. In research with urban schools, Ainscow and West (2006: 137) found headteachers were beginning to identify shared 'principles around which their staff could be drawn together'. This was generating a new impetus for change across schools, wider ownership of the improvement agenda and reduced polarization. They conclude that, despite the longer-term deepening of socio-economic inequalities by market reforms, there are reasons for optimism as 'the system has considerable untapped potential to improve itself' (2006: 131). This exists in the accumulated skills, knowledge and creativity within and between schools and their local communities.

Putting these resources to the task of improving outcomes beyond the individual school is a challenging but vital leadership task. Resolving tensions between collaboration and competition will demand leadership of people and organizations beyond restrictive institutional boundaries and cultures. Systems of collaborative organization may start to complicate formal structures (Bentley 2003). But tapping 'system potential' holds out the promise of far-reaching progressive effects on the nature of schooling. Through extending school leadership beyond the insular school unit, schools acting collaboratively can take greater joint responsibility for the life chances of a wider community of young people.

Top-down versus bottom-up

This is a very different vision of school leadership to that implied by a range of government policies and external accountabilities. It also implies some appropriation of decision-making power by the school or school collaborative – at least in pooling or aggregating school-level resources to take risks, innovate and lead a renewal of learning and social inclusion from within schools.

Debates over effective forms of system organization, leadership and local autonomy have gathered pace since the turn of the millennium. A range of analyses can be traced to the plateau in student attainment as recorded by the national tests in English primary schools between 2001 and 2004. This followed several years of impressive system-wide improvements from 1997 which had been driven by central government policy. This included the Primary National Strategy (previously the National Literacy and National Numeracy Strategies), clear external targets and substantial new investment. For many, the subsequent plateau in attainment was evidence that rapid increases in attainment through central prescription could never be sustainable in the longer run (Hargreaves and Fink 2006). The argument goes something like this:

- Most agreed that standards were too low and too varied in the 1970s and 1980s and that some form of direct state intervention was necessary. The resultant national prescription proved successful, particularly in raising standards in primary schools – progress confirmed by international comparisons.

- But progress plateaued and, while a bit more improvement has continued to be squeezed out nationally since 2004, and considerably more in underperforming schools, one has to question whether prescription still offers the recipe for sustained large-scale reform into the medium or longer term.
- There is a growing recognition that schools need to lead the next phase of reform. But, if the hypothesis is correct, and this is much contested terrain, it must categorically not be a naïve return to the not so halcyon days of the 1970s when a thousand flowers bloomed and the educational life chances of too many of our children wilted.

Getting beyond this top-down approach, while avoiding the limitations of highly decentralized strategies, was the purpose of Michael Fullan's (2004a, 2004b) seminal work on 'system leaders in action'. The priority, he argued, was to 'reconcile the power and action of the centre, with the ideas, wisdom and engagement of the field' (2004a: 6). Three key principles were offered for doing so: first, the fostering of a collective commitment in which the centre, local government and schools moved towards mutual influence; second, following David Hargreaves (2003), the widespread development of networks that enable the lateral transfer of disciplined innovation between schools; third, the mobilization of a critical mass of leaders at all levels of the system who work intensely in their own organizations and, at the same time, participate in the bigger picture.

This draws on Peter Senge's (1990) notion of 'system thinking' with the implication that leaders need to look beyond their own discrete activity to consider wider interconnections through which they can collectively lead change. In this way, the central state needs to play a more enabling role. School leaders need to take direct action by sharing knowledge and learning with other schools and by taking on explicit assignments to promote system improvement (Fullan 2004a: 14–15). A key indicator is 'when individual school heads become almost as concerned about the success of other schools as they are about their own school' (2004a: 9).

This is perhaps the most appropriate guiding motif for a growing number of school leaders whom we have termed 'system leaders'. But if system leaders are to provide a solution to the problems of top-down reform, the test should be whether they can create the conditions for a new professionalism. In particular, such professionalism should be capable of harnessing local ownership and ideas and measuring success in terms of improving student learning and well-being and tackling inequalities.

A new professionalism

The concept of 'professionalism' is much politicized. Historically, the welfare state professional of the post-war era became maligned as new social movements around the 1960s, and later consumerism, challenged the passive exclusion of individual decision-making by professionals 'who knew best' (Ranson 1994). Not all public sector employees had the skills to use their privileged position professionally (Kogan 1994). The response, most clearly in education from the 1980s, marked the start of a gradual but steady erosion of government trust in the public sector professional. While control over resources flowed to school leadership and management, this new autonomy was greatly tempered by a significant centralization of decision-making over the curriculum, assessment and accountability.

Two highlights of a continuing contemporary impulse to centrally prescribe include, first, a constant stream of initiatives that schools have been either required or encouraged to implement.[3] These have often been shown to sap the time and energy of teachers and heads (Coffield 2007). Second, and perhaps more importantly, the pressure of external accountability which accompanied the drive for rapid increases in attainment, as measured by tests and examinations, has been heavily criticized for creating a climate of mistrust and perverting the purposes of education. This has been shown to encourage teachers to 'teach to the test' and schools to covertly adjust their admissions policies in order to boost their position in performance tables (Ball 2003).

These critical perspectives are somewhat complicated by the discernible shift during this period from schooling as a 'secret garden' towards a greater willingness of teachers to discuss their instructional practice. Some, often newer, teachers, who did not experience the freedoms of the 1970s, also report seeing the National Curriculum as having provided a shared language with colleagues and a structure in which to be creative. Yet the overriding sense is that of a reduced autonomy for teachers rather than a respect for their creativity (Hargreaves 2003: 57). Indeed, the calls for change have now come to centre stage in British politics. The 'new' Conservative Party has sought to move on to traditional Labour ground by positioning itself as a champion of high quality public services and by employing a discourse of setting the professional free to respond to local need.

The implication is that we need a transition from an era of prescription to an era of professionalism – in which the balance between national prescription and schools leading reform will change. Achieving this shift is not straightforward. We cannot simply move from one era to the other without self-consciously building professional capacity throughout the system. This was a central argument of David Hopkins's (2007a) *Every School a Great School* and it is this progression that is illustrated in Figure 1.1.

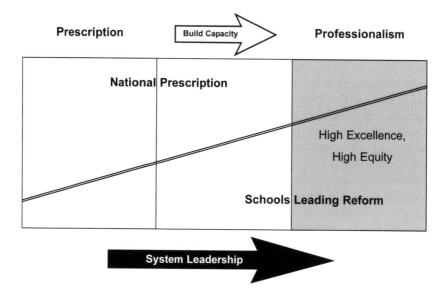

Figure 1.1 From prescription to professionalism

It is worth taking a little time to consider the thinking underlying the diagram. Several points need to be made. First, it must be emphasized that this is not an argument against top-down change per se. Neither top-down nor bottom-up change work just by themselves; they have to be in balance – in creative tension. The balance between the two at any one time will depend, of course, on context.

Second, the left hand segment of the diagram reflects the significant centralism in England during the 1990s. If we assume that time moves from left to right in the diagram, then it is most probably correct to say that, in terms of both policy and practice, England is currently located in the middle segment of the diagram. This is contested terrain and there is no guarantee that there will be an inevitable movement into the right hand segment although, as we have seen, the portents currently look good.

Third, it should be no surprise to realize that the right hand segment is relatively unknown territory. Professional capacity implies a rebalancing towards greater internal evaluation, a much deeper and wider development of learning communities, widespread horizontal and lateral ways of working and, above all, the leadership of learning by schools. The difficulty is that, in imagining this new professionalism, the thinking of many stakeholders is constrained by their experiences within the existing power structure.

Fourth, we believe it is leadership, more precisely system leadership, which will ultimately provide the energy and dynamism to move from an era of prescription to one of professionalism. Despite the rhetoric of politicians and civil servants, both local and national, their default position is too often to maintain their authority and by that token the *status quo*. They may talk about devolution but their instincts, particularly in education, are to retain central control.

The emergence of system leadership

If this, then, is the traditional status quo, the system leadership thesis of change is given greater credibility by recent moves in policy towards more professional judgement. Two highlights[4] include, first, the Every Child Matters (ECM) agenda, with the expectation it places on local authorities to coordinate children's services better so that it is easier for a range of (multi-agency) professionals to work together to improve the well-being of young people. Second, there is the emphasis of the New Relationship with Schools on bottom-up target-setting and direct support for school leaders by School Improvement Partners (SIPs), many of whom are or have been peer head-teachers. The detail of some these new policies, particularly around ECM, extended services and communities, has been summarized by Collarbone and West-Burnham (2008).

It is difficult to identify when exactly these moves in policy originated, but it is certain that system leadership has been positively advocated by government Ministers over the past four years. Perhaps the earliest and most committed was David Miliband MP. When Minister of State for School Standards, Miliband saw that the development and deployment of a cadre of system leaders could go a long way to responding to the key challenges he had identified for school leadership as part of a new relationship between schools and government (Miliband 2004). This included raising productivity in education, effecting greater social justice and ensuring more sustainable improvement (Miliband 2003).

This was then endorsed in policy in the 2005 White Paper *Higher Standards, Better Schools for All* (DfES 2005a: 99–101) that included the government's intention to:

- encourage the growth of federations and other partnership arrangements which ensure our most successful school leaders are used to best effect and are able to support our less successful schools;
- ask the [National] College [for School Leadership] to identify, with the help of a range of partners, a new group of national leaders of education, drawn from those who are succeeding in our most challenging leadership roles;
- [require] these top head teachers [to] work closely with the College to influence the direction and targeting of leadership provision across

the school system. They will also be able to advise Ministers on the future direction of education policy on the basis of their expert experience;

- develop better career paths for school leaders who have the talent and experience to be considered as national leaders of education; those with the ability to run our most challenging schools.

Over subsequent years the government has reiterated its commitment to developing system leadership and collaboration in, for instance, the Children's Plan (DCSF 2007a) and the National Challenge (DCSF 2008a). Most significant, however, is the emergence of a growing number of roles in which school leaders can actually act as system leaders *in practice*. This has been a fast-moving context. In 2004, Fullan's two concrete examples of 'system thinkers in action' were: Primary Strategy Consultant leaders; and local authority directors enabling school headteachers to interact with each other to help shape their locality. Four years on, we have witnessed rapid growth in both centrally mandated and locally developed system leadership activity. Examples now include leadership of: a wide range of local and more egalitarian collaboratives, Leading Edge partnerships and federations; 14 to 19 consortia and networks of extended provision; SIPs and National Leaders of Education (NLEs); and, at the teacher leader level, Advanced Skills Teachers. As we shall explore in Chapter 2, it is not the named roles themselves but, rather, what leaders do through them that constitutes system leadership. But, from a small start, these roles appear to have the potential to grow into a professional movement.

The system leadership thesis that we explore in this book is that the outstanding practice of system leaders and their schools can continue to drive policy further into new areas of professional autonomy. By being willing and able to work for the success and well-being of students in other schools as well as their own, these leaders can show how self-managed schools, emerging from an era of competition, might work together for greater social equity. By seeing collaboration with other schools and agencies as vital to delivering on aims that individual schools cannot achieve by themselves, system leaders can create alternative solutions to a range of educational challenges that have traditionally become the responsibility and preserve of central government. By starting from the problems and solutions of schools themselves, rather than those identified by others, system leaders can show how professionals might take more control of educational reform and contribute directly to a broader renewal of the education system.

System management

Not all see it this way. There is the argument that new nationally developed and administered leadership roles, such as SIPs or Primary Strategy Consultant Leaders, are, in fact, only extensions of the state's prescriptive arm. The aspiration is less a new professionalism and more local management of national performance targets (Carole Whitty[5], personal communication, October 2007). These critiques point to the burdensome accountability functions of SIPs, the alleged new 'independence' for state schools that focuses on governance structures rather than curricular freedoms, and to covert state pressure. Indeed, we have found qualitative evidence that, beyond its own sponsored pilots, the government may be exerting pressure on local authorities to federate low-achieving schools with higher-performing neighbours – with the threat of their otherwise missing out on multi-million pound capital investments promised in the Building Schools for the Future programme.

This is expanded on by Hatcher (2008) who argues that networks of schools can serve either 'new participatory relations' between teachers or 'the transmission of government agendas' (2008: 29). In the latter form, networks have to be managed to ensure that they align with government agendas and so local system managers are required. Hatcher also draws on Jessop's (2002) notion of 'heterarchy' which is defined as horizontal self-organization between system actors. For Jessop, the state is increasingly interested in these network forms as they may enhance its 'capacity to secure political objectives by sharing power with or delegating to forces beyond it' (2002: 237). In short, for Hatcher, professional networks provide the state with another system management tool within the standards agenda, with system leaders cast as a 'new super-managerial elite'.

Concerns over local management of central policy in education of course have a longer history. Hoyle and Wallace (2005, 2007) trace this back to Prime Minister James Callaghan's Ruskin speech in 1976 and his critique of the autonomous public sector professional. The subsequent development of bureaucratic accountability has diverted teachers away from their core task of teaching. But Hoyle and Wallace offer some hope for local agency as 'in order to meet the perceived needs of their pupils, head teachers and teachers adapt national policy while at the same time appearing to implement these policies with fidelity' (2007: 17). This irony in the tension between prescription and professionalism has led to disillusionment among some school leaders. Others, however, have fashioned their own local approaches by being 'flexible and opportunistic' but also 'principled' in weighing external reforms against the needs of their pupils.

This seems to clarify what many of us may have found implicit. To function authentically most schools and their leaders need to retain a subversive dimension. For us, this extends to system leadership. There are probably already schools around the country developing elements of system management that co-exist alongside system leadership in practice: the SIPs who create time for professional support rather than being overwhelmed by accountability tasks; the schools using their joint capacity and purpose to build more equitable provision for a locality while still operating within the quasi-market. Given that we are still within the pre-existing centralist paradigm, such evidence of both narratives is surely to be expected. This is perhaps exemplified best by the recently announced National Challenge. This has the ambitious aim of ensuring all secondary schools have at least 30 per cent of their GCSE students achieving 5 A*–C grades including English and Maths by 2011. It is still an emerging policy but it appears to both incentivize system leaders to work for improvement in lower achieving schools while simultaneously prescribing a great deal of how this will happen. Its launch was also potentially damaging to the very schools it wants to support, by publishing their names and enabling the media to compile lists of 'failing schools' threatened with closure (Rogers 2008). For the foreseeable future, therefore, it is probable that many school leaders will continue to work between these contradictions of government-led reform and locally-led renewal.

Purpose of this book

In this book we analyse specific cases of the emergence of *system leadership in practice*. We attempt to detail:

- whether and how school and system resources are being mobilized collaboratively by schools for their mutual benefit;
- if so, how such system leadership is undertaken and what common skills and characteristics are employed in doing so;
- what impact this has on outcomes for students;
- whether this constitutes the basis for a new professionalism and a relocation of power from the centre.

In pursuing this analysis, we present evidence of the experiences of a range of schools and partnerships that are charting new ground. We focus on schools and school leaders. This leads, we recognize, to a partial perspective, with system leaders within local authorities and national agencies remaining only a secondary focus where they appear in partnership with school leaders. Our rationale for this focus is threefold. First, and inevitably, a significant part of the capacity for change exists with the 23,000 schools themselves that constitute the system. Second, if the system leadership thesis is to be believed, it is school intelligence and practice that will lead to change. Third, for a new professionalism to occur, it will require a multitude of new lateral interactions between schools to rebalance or rival the central power structure.

While demonstrating counter-perspectives, and recognizing that our account errs towards successful instances of a new phenomenon, our primary argument is that there is substantial evidence of system leadership as an emerging practice. This does not appear to be widespread at present, but it does represent a powerful new means for professionals to work together to improve student outcomes. We progress our argument and analysis in three main ways.

First, in Chapter 2, we draw on a national questionnaire to map, quantify and further define the current landscape of system leadership. Having established an understanding of the scales at which such activity is being undertaken, we propose five distinct yet overlapping categories of system leadership. These are conceptualized, as we alluded to at the start of this chapter as: leadership of sustained improvements in very challenging contexts; leadership of collaborative innovations in curriculum and pedagogy; leadership that brokers and shapes radically new networks of extended services; leadership of improvement across a formal partnership of schools; leadership that acts as an external agent of change in other schools that face difficulties.

Second, in the subsequent five chapters (3 to 7), we explore each of these roles in detail. In each case we draw on research we have undertaken over the last three years to analyse the skills, tasks and characteristics that appear to be implicated in system leadership. We also have a close eye on the impact of this new work on outcomes for students. To retain narrative drive, we do not discuss the methodological implications of each chapter in much detail. We refer interested readers to our earlier publications. In presenting our research, we have also deliberately used a number of narrative styles to respond best to the contexts in which we have worked.

In Chapter 3, we focus on schools that have sustained improvement for about a decade in challenging circumstances. We provide detailed evidence of how these schools have achieved these transformations. We argue that, in having truly changed the contexts in which their staff teach and their students learn, these schools are contributing to system change: by providing an exemplar of how student outcomes can be improved; and by then sharing this intelligence with other schools locally. Indeed, each of the schools is now taking on additional system roles that seek to lead improvements in their locality. We are interested in why these new roles have been developed and what it is that each school brings to the task.

In Chapter 4, we analyse schools and leaders who work across partnerships and networks to share innovations in teaching and learning, curriculum and assessment. We focus on Leading Edge partnerships as a case study for our analysis and explore the main themes and impact of such work. We find both a focus on innovating personalized learning strategies and an emerging set of positive outcomes. We exemplify a number of collaborative working practices and also propose a model of how schools might work together with greater rigour. The skills and tasks that appear to be implicated in such system leadership include new approaches to capacity-building, lateral account-ability to sustain progress and a partnership ethos that supports mutual improvement.

In Chapter 5, we show how system leadership in the context of ECM can be conceived as brokering and shaping networks of provision across local schools, local agencies and communities so as to personalize social care and education for individual students and their families. This is exemplified across the 0 to 19 age range and a new classification of school-community relationships is also proposed. The ECM agenda, we argue, has shifted the focus of the school in its community from informal community links and – in some schools – provision of community education to a clear focus on children, young people and parenting, and coherent multi-agency support.

In Chapter 6, we elaborate the concepts of support federations and executive headship. We explore the historical and policy contexts from which these roles have developed before analysing not only how such roles are being undertaken but also what forms of expertise are mobilized in the pursuit of another school's improvement. To summarize this, we propose a framework of practice that includes the lead school's capacity, the new leadership model developed, how the partnership is designed, the nature of the improvement process and how knowledge is transferred. We conclude by considering whether federations and these new leadership roles can provide alternative solutions to problems that have traditionally become the responsibility and preserve of the central apparatus of the state.

In Chapter 7, we develop the concepts of change agents with reference to both consultant leaders and NLEs. We consider the contexts out of which these national roles are developing. We then illustrate the characteristics of such leaders, how they work at a system level and how their schools provide operational support to other schools. We analyse early evidence of their impact and consider the effectiveness of these approaches in school intervention, support and improvement.

Third and finally, in Chapter 8, we seek to pull together the evidence presented in each empirical chapter and consider the overall implications for the system leadership thesis. In doing so, we are encouraged enough to suggest that we may well be heading towards a transformative moment in which dominant forms of top-down control are re-balanced by more lateral forms of support and accountability. While recognizing that this may represent a relatively optimistic position, we outline a number of themes that summarize this perspective. First, we argue that system leadership at all levels is vital if we are to renew and deepen the teaching and learning process and engage students authentically in doing so. Second, we recast the system leadership/ system management dialectic as a spectrum or continuum of overlapping roles that may in fact be necessary to move us from an era of prescription to one where schools play a greater role in leading reform. Third, we argue that the ability to transfer innovation and proven practice from one school to others is a key component of system leadership in practice. However, if this is to be developed at a wider scale, new forms of partnership, support and intervention need to be provided increasingly by schools themselves, rather than being imposed by some external agency. On this basis we make a number of policy recommendations. Fourth, we show how a 'system imperative' is not an isolated educational or even English phenomenon but part of a broader public and global reform. Finally, we argue that system leadership is not an isolated activity engaged in by a few idiosyncratic 'hero innovators'. Rather it is our overarching claim that system leadership has the characteristics of an emerging movement, focused on *both* achieving as high a level of learning for individual students as possible *and on* promoting social justice.

2 Mapping the system leadership landscape

We have defined system leaders as those school leaders who are willing to shoulder wider system roles in order to support the improvement of other schools as well as their own. Until very recently, there has been little attempt to document how such leadership is evolving and being enacted across the English education system. This chapter elaborates the concept of system leadership and illustrates its potential as a catalyst for systemic reform in three main ways. First, it extends the initial conceptualization of system leadership developed in the previous chapter and then raises a series of concerns about the way the concept is being interpreted. Second, by drawing on survey responses provided by local authorities, the then Department for Education and Skills (DfES) and a range of national agencies and professional associations, it maps the current landscape of system leadership. From this analysis, a five part taxonomy is proposed of the roles that system leaders are currently assuming. This taxonomy provides the organizing framework for the subsequent Chapters 3 to 7. Third, and based on these analyses and research with school leaders, this chapter proposes a potential model for system leadership and explores the tensions involved in developing the concept further.

Defining system leadership

As is becoming clear, the concept of 'system leadership' is one that has recently caught the educational imagination. Take, for example, these quotations from two significant opinion-makers: the first from the General Secretary of the Association of School and College Leaders in England and the other from a leading educational commentator whose work has a global reach.

John Dunford (2005), in an address to the National Conference of the Specialist Schools and Academies Trust (SSAT), argued that:

> The greatest challenge on our leadership journey is how we can bring about system improvement. How can we contribute to the raising of standards, not only in our own school, but in others, and colleges too? What types of leaders are needed for this task? What style of

leadership is required if we are to achieve the sea-change in performance that is demanded of us?

In *System Thinkers in Action* Michael Fullan (2004a: 7) argued that:

> A new kind of leadership is necessary to break through the status quo. Systematic forces, sometimes called inertia, have the upper hand in preventing system shifts. Therefore, it will take powerful, proactive forces to change the existing system (to change context). This can be done directly and indirectly through systems thinking in action. These new theoreticians are leaders who work intensely in their own schools, or national agencies, and at the same time connect with and participate in the bigger picture. To change organizations and systems will require leaders to get experience in linking other parts of the system. These leaders in turn must help develop other leaders within similar characteristics.

These quotations share three implicit assumptions. The first is that if we are ever to achieve sustainable education change, it must be led by those close to the school; the second is that this must have a systemic focus; and the third is that 'system leadership' is an emerging practice.

These assumptions lead to three other observations, discussed in detail in this chapter. The first is that there is a tension between system leadership as a national policy or a professional movement. This dichotomy, as we will see, has profound implications for the prospect of sustainable educational reform. The second is that, although system leadership is emerging as a professional practice, it is a concept that is located in a rich theoretical and research context. The conceptual concerns of system theory for relationships, structures and interdependencies (Katz and Kahn 1966; Senge 1990; Campbell et al. 1994) underpin the contemporary work of system leaders in practice. The third observation is that, as we have already noted, while most school leaders in England are involved in some form of collaborative activity or networking, this is categorically not the same as system leadership. System leadership, in the sense it is used in this book, implies a significantly more substantive engagement with other schools or agencies in order to bring about system transformation.

Taken together, this suggests that system leadership is a concept whose time has come. One can summarize these views by saying that system leadership is increasingly being seen as:

- a wider resource for school innovation and improvement, making more of our most successful leaders by encouraging and enabling them to: identify and transfer best practice; reduce the risk of innovation in other schools; and lead partnerships that improve and diversify educational pathways for students within and across localities;

- a more authentic response to low attaining schools. Currently, schools in special measures[1] or with a notice to improve are responsible for approximately 300,000 pupils. Strong leadership is vital to turn these schools around. However, a central challenge is that these schools are often the least able to attract suitable leaders. Our most successful school leaders hold the potential to have an impact on these schools, which need their expertise, by working to develop and mobilize leadership capacity in the pursuit of whole-school improvement;

- a potential means to resolve, in the longer term, the emerging and related challenges of a declining supply of well qualified school leaders, falling student rolls and, hence, increasingly non-viable schools, and yet continuing pressures to sustain educational provision in all localities.

This latter point is important. The current declining supply of school leaders relates to a high proportion of headteachers nearing retirement age coupled with a lack of aspirant deputies. Gronn (2003) argues that this trend is underpinned by a broader 'disengagement from leadership' as teachers abstain from taking on leadership posts, leading to projected shortages and recurring recruitment difficulties. The National College for School Leadership (NCSL 2006) suggests that system leadership solutions may include fewer headteachers across some groups of schools, new challenges and incentives for the retention of the most experienced headteachers, as well as new development opportunities for deputies and middle leaders to experience aspects of headship at first hand before taking on full headteacher responsibilities.

Before we get too carried away, however, with enthusiasm for the concept of system leadership, we need to admit that much of this well intentioned advocacy is based on aspiration and a few early individual cases rather than systemic evidence. Despite its attractiveness as a new catalyst for system change, there is a range of challenges to be faced if we are to avoid a simplified and uncritical approach to system leadership. We have several concerns. First, there is currently no clear or systemic knowledge of how leaders undertake system leadership roles. Second, there is now only beginning to be evidence of effectiveness, including on the proportion of system leaders who are successful, their impact in different contexts and what might constitute best practice. Much of this is reported in this book. Third, there is no certainty that sufficient leadership quality and, crucially, whole-school capacity exist on which to build a wide range of effective and sustainable system leadership roles. Fourth, it is not always clear how capacity is renewed within the schools from which system leaders work, especially those in challenging circumstances. Fifth, there is no consensus about how best (or who is best placed) to deploy and develop a range of existing and aspirant system leaders to ensure that they gain the skills, experience and support needed to be effective. The recent announcement of the National Challenge, of course, may change this. Sixth, as was seen in Chapter 1, there is a wider debate within the school leader profession about how to reconcile, on the one hand, an impetus for collaboration between schools with, on the other hand, an accountability system focused on individual schools (which has the potential to act as an impetus for competition). This perceived tension certainly does not restrict nascent system leadership, but it is considered an important contextual dimension in which wider systemic roles are being developed.

Above all, and perhaps most significantly, it is not actually clear what or how many system leadership roles are being undertaken. Possibly as a result of being a relatively new professional practice, there appears to have been little attempt so far to document how system leadership is being enacted and is evolving across the English education system. In an attempt to correct this, we report in this chapter on research that provides an initial perspective on its nature and extent. To do so we provide, first, a snapshot of identified activity in June 2006, now updated for this book in September 2008; second, we set out a taxonomy of system leadership roles; and third, we propose an outline conceptualization and model of what effective system leaders do.

To map the current landscape, an e-questionnaire was sent to every local authority in England, the then DfES, a range of national agencies and associations[2] and a number of networks of school leaders. Respondents were asked to identify school leaders taking on wider systemic roles beyond their own school. A response was gained from 76 local authorities (about 50 per cent), as well as from all the national agencies and networks contacted. A small random sample of these responses was validated directly with individual schools. To test these data and consider the leadership strategies and challenges involved, two whole-day research seminars were held with a total of 50 existing and aspirant system leaders. The seminars focused on facilitated discussion structured around the four emerging themes of roles and strategies; agency and brokerage; professional capacity and development; and accountability, funding and systemic reform.

Mapping the landscape

A first glance at a map of the landscape shows a significant amount of activity taking place. The total number of system leaders identified by respondents across all phases was 1313. This points to about 5 or 6 per cent of school leaders already engaged in some form of system leadership activity. While this is an initial snapshot, what does seem certain is that system leadership may be thought of as an emerging professional movement rather than an elite practice of a very few 'super-heads'. This widespread nature is borne out by the fact that every local authority had at least a few system leaders, with several containing many more.

Exploring this distribution further, an important division emerges in the nature and geographic scale at which different roles are organized and undertaken. Simply put, a division exists between school leaders undertaking roles created on a *national* scale, predominantly within the ambit of government-led programmes, and those taking on roles developed at a *local* level as a result of a professional commitment to wider change.

As is evident in Table 2.1, the majority of identified system leaders fall into the 'nationally developed' grouping. These include consultant leaders, National Leaders of Education, School Improvement Partners, mentor heads and leaders of Leading Edge partnerships. This group shares several key characteristics. First, the impetus and agency behind the roles are located at a national level, often within the Department for Children, Schools and Families (DCSF) – including the National Strategies, or the NCSL. Second, the focus is on deploying the knowledge and skills of experienced headteachers and other leaders as part of a broader school improvement, leadership support or innovation programme. Third, a funding schedule is provided for continuing professional development (CPD), salary payment, supply cover and so forth. And fourth, the roles themselves are relatively standardized through entry requirements and selection procedures, clear protocols for action set out in guidance, and an evaluation system to monitor progress.

Table 2.1 The extent of system leadership activity in England in 2008

System leadership roles[3]	Number
Executive Headship/Leader of a Federation	101
Support for a school facing difficulties	81
Leading Community/Multi-Agency partnerships	78
Improvement in challenging contexts, including Academies	83
Leaders of Leading Edge partnerships[4]	212
Consultant Leaders[5]	134
Mentor Heads	139
School Improvement Partners	255
National Leaders of Education[6]	200
Others, including all-through schools and amalgamations	49
Total[7]	1313

The second grouping of roles consists of those developed predominantly at a local level. These include many executive headteachers, less formalized support partnerships, the leadership of local networks and sustained improvement in challenging circumstances. While less numerous, these roles appear to be as significant. For, while centrally-driven roles establish a wide coverage in a relatively short time, locally developed roles often emerge less quickly due to the need to work through local bureaucracy and possible opposition. Indeed, the shared characteristics of these roles are that they are flexible, organic and, often, initially ad hoc. While aligned to national priorities of school improvement and student welfare, local responsiveness is a critical element in how these roles come about and how such leaders work to reform (local) systems. With such flexibility and local variation, there are often complex and contextually specific answers to questions about who takes the initiative for a school leader to become a system leader and who makes key decisions at a local level. But such complexity is not seen to undermine the potential effectiveness of such roles. For example, as the NCSL argued three years ago in its advice on complex schools to the Secretary of State for Education: 'there is a growing body of evidence from around the country that, where a school is in serious trouble, the use of an executive head teacher/ partner head teacher and a paired arrangement with that head's successful school, can be a particularly effective solution, and is being increasingly widely applied' (NCSL 2005b: 3).

Taxonomy of Roles

Having established a map of the landscape and an understanding of the scales at which such activity is being undertaken, it is important, at this stage, to reflect on how best we might describe and theorize this emerging range of roles. For, while diverse, they all share the guiding principle of system leadership, of working for the success and welfare of students in other schools, as well as their own. Our research points to five distinct yet overlapping categories of system leadership and leads us to propose the following taxonomy.

First, there are leaders who **_sustain improvement in a school in extremely challenging circumstances_** and then share their knowledge and practice with other schools. A key objective of system leadership is to 'change contexts' in our most challenging circumstances. These leaders choose to lead and improve low-achieving schools and then develop the capability to sustain them as high value-added institutions over a significant period of time. In doing so, they are well placed to share their knowledge, skills and experience to help similar local schools to improve. Crucially, this can provide a professionally led route to achieve what Elmore (2004: 253) defines as 'the means to make sure that help gets to the right schools at the right time with the right technical expertise'. Indeed, it is from such experiences that the NLEs (see Chapter 7) have emerged.

Second, there are leaders who develop and *lead a successful innovation and improvement partnership* across several schools. These are most usually focused on a set of specific themes that have clear outcomes and reach beyond the capacity of any single institution. Examples include partnerships on curriculum design and specialisms, pedagogic innovation and 14 to 19 pathways. Rather than needing one school to have developed the skill and capacity to (help) lead the improvement of another, it is more clearly focused on two or more schools working jointly on issues of mutual interest and challenge. These partnerships often remain in what are commonly referred to as 'soft' organizational collaboratives. However some have moved to 'harder' more formalized arrangements in the form of (co-)federations (to develop stronger mechanisms for joint governance and accountability) or Education Improvement Partnerships (to formalize the devolution of defined delivery responsibilities and resources from their local authority; DfES 2005b). As a result of recent legislation, such groupings now have the possibility of forming independent School Trusts.

Third, there are *leaders working in the context of ECM* to broker and shape partnerships or networks of wider relationships across local communities to support children's welfare and learning. Such leadership is also firmly rooted within the context of national Children's Plans and the extended schools agenda. Matthews (2006a) conceives four key dimensions to this work: organizing resources for learning from the community; widening learning experiences beyond the school; drawing support for child and family welfare into the school or network; and providing for the lifelong learning needs of the community. This often includes the leadership of multi-agency work.

Fourth, there are leaders who *partner another school facing difficulties and improve it*. This includes both executive headteachers and leaders of more informal improvement arrangements who work from their lead school with a low-achieving or underperforming school (or schools) that requires significant support or intervention. Executive headteachers provide an example. They are responsible for two or more schools that have either entered into a federation or a local (often time-bound) agreement focused on a lead school working to improve a partner. The potential for these roles is provided for in legislation (Education Act, DfES 2002a) and the government sponsors 37 pilot federations, several of which are run by executive heads. However, often, the driving force behind these roles is located locally and, as such, can vary. For instance, where one partnership may be developed closely with a local authority, another may result from its perceived inertia. This flexibility also extends to how executive headteachers operate. There is no guidance, additional accountability, professional development or centrally located funding stream.

Fifth, there are leaders who work as a ***change agent*** or expert leader. The focus is on providing practical knowledge and guidance as well as the transfer of best practice within a formalized school improvement programme. This currently includes roles that exist within centrally organized programmes such as consultant leaders, National Leaders of Education and School Improvement Partners.

What effective system leaders do

We have now explored a range of system leadership roles and established a taxonomy of the five key areas of identified activity. We have also seen some emerging evidence of the effectiveness of system leadership, with regard to specific roles and objectives. What seems increasingly important is how system leaders actually work to achieve these objectives – for, as we are keenly aware, their work often enters new territories that have novel challenges and no well rehearsed solutions. The purpose of the following five chapters is to explore in some depth the activities underpinning the five roles we have just identified.

Before embarking on this endeavour we thought it helpful to begin to set out a conceptual framework in which to consider this range of system leadership activity. We referred briefly in Chapter 1 to systems theory. The literature in this area provides a direction of travel. The key insight has been well summarized by Kofman and Senge (1995: 27) when they state that the 'defining characteristic of a system is that it cannot be understood as a function of its isolated components. ... the system doesn't depend on what each part is doing but on how each part is interacting with the rest'. This leads to the realization, intimated earlier, that in order to maximize the value of systems theory one not only needs to utilize a system thinking perspective, but also to view it within the context of a learning organization. This, in turn, requires the assiduous development of the range of skills associated with system leadership to transform not only the organization but also the system as a whole.

An important perspective on this skill set is offered by Heifetz (1994) through the concept of 'adaptive leadership'. His argument is that leaders increasingly require skills that move beyond traditional management solutions for technical problems to provide adaptive responses to challenges 'without easy answers'. Technical problems, such as how to teach numeracy, and their solutions of course will remain vital. But system leaders will also need to work adaptively to lead people and organizations beyond restrictive boundaries, perceived wisdoms and entrenched cultures where they exist as obstacles to improvement.

This theme, as we saw earlier, underpins Fullan's (2004b) exposition of the role he believes school leaders will need to play as 'system thinkers in action' if sustainable large-scale reform is to be achieved. This, Fullan argues, will necessarily involve adaptive challenges that 'require the deep participation of the people with the problem; [and] that is why it is more complex and why it requires more sophisticated leadership' (2004b: 53). For Fullan, examples of this new work include: leading and facilitating a revolution in pedagogy; understanding and changing the culture of a school for the better; relating to the broader community, in particular with parents, and integrating and coordinating the work of social service agencies into the school as a hub (2004b: 57–61). This will demand: 'above all … powerful strategies that enable people to question and alter certain values and beliefs as they create new forms of learning within and between schools, and across levels of the system' (2004b: 60).

Such demands are further illuminated in theory by Peter Senge (1990: 3) who argues that, for organizations to excel, they have to become 'learning organizations', which he defines as: 'organizations where people continually expand their capacity to create the results they truly desire, where new and expansive patterns of thinking are nurtured, where collective aspiration is set free, and where people are continually learning to see the whole together'. To Senge, the key to becoming a 'learning organization' is for leaders to tap into people's commitment and capacity to learn at all levels, so that broader systemic interdependencies and how to change them effectively can be made clearer (1990: 4).

There is a loud and clear read-across here from system theory to the key areas of system leadership activity we have already identified. There is also a sense of a shared, central set of skills that system leaders need to be effective which reflects the established literature on educational leadership (for a comprehensive review see Leithwood et al. 1999). There is, however, a real concern about the increasing tendency in the literature to distort the generic competencies of leaders through celebrating singular aspects of the role. Leithwood and his colleagues (2004: 4) express this worry succinctly: 'we need to be skeptical about the "leadership by adjective" literature. Sometimes these adjectives have real meaning, but sometimes they mask the more important themes common to successful leadership, regardless of the style being advocated.'

These are wise words and, of course, we ourselves are in danger of being hoisted by our own petard. In our defence, we would claim that the concept of 'system leadership' is embracing rather than esoteric. This claim is made on three grounds. First, the concept of system leadership, as we have seen, locates itself within the general literature on systems theory and thinking and, as such, is inclusive rather than exclusive. Second, as we see shortly, 'system leadership' is a 'theory of action' that embraces a catholic range of disciplines in order to exert its power (see, for example, Elmore 2004;

Leithwood et al. 2006). And, as we hope is becoming clear, system leadership will exert an influence only to the extent that it focuses on teaching and learning (that is, is instructional), shares its authority with others (that is, is distributed) and so on. To reiterate, system leadership as a concept is integrative rather than exclusive.

This discussion emphasizes the focus on the key capabilities required by system leaders. Inevitably this demands the development of hypotheses as we move inductively from our data. To do so, we have found it helpful to draw on Leithwood and Riehl's (2003) core leadership practices in proposing an initial outline of the key capabilities which system leaders appear to bring to their role. This is set out in Table 2.2. Building on these key capabilities, and combining them with the range of identified roles, it is possible to offer a model of system leadership practice that emerges inductively from the actions of leaders we have researched. This is set out in Figure 2.1 where the model exhibits a logic that flows from the inside outwards. At the centre, leaders, driven by a moral purpose related to the enhancement of student learning, seek to empower teachers and others to make schools a critical force for improving communities. This is premised on the argument already made, namely that sustainable educational development requires educational leaders who are willing to shoulder broader leadership roles: who care about and work for the success of other schools as well as their own. In relation to the concept of moral purpose, it should be stressed that school leaders are not system leaders simply because of the role they play but because of the values, commitment and approach they bring to the task.

It is also clear from our research that system leaders share a characteristic set of behaviours and skills. As illustrated in the second inner ring of the diagram, these are of two types. First, system leaders engage in personal development, usually informally through benchmarking themselves against their peers and developing their skill base in response to the context they find themselves working in. Although there is a strong similarity in these aptitudes and skills to the national standards for headship, the system leaders we have seen have moved beyond or transcended the standards and, in going deeper, have integrated them into a personal style. Second, all the system leaders we have studied have a strategic capability; they are able to translate their vision or moral purpose into operational principles that have tangible outcomes. Taken together, these two inner circles of the diagram reflect the core practice of 'setting direction', as noted in Table 2.2.

As is denoted in the third ring of the model, the moral purpose, personal qualities and strategic capacity of the system leader find focus in the three domains of the school: managing the teaching and learning process, developing people, and developing the organization. Here the focus on student learning and achievement is paramount. Each of the three domains links together to provide a powerful infrastructure for student learning.

Table 2.2 A conceptualization of the key capabilities for system leaders

Core practices	Leadership capabilities	System leadership implications
1 Setting direction	Total commitment to enable all learners to reach their potential with a strategic vision that extends into the future and brings immediacy to the delivery of improvements for students.	Translation of vision into whole-school programmes that extend the impact of pedagogic and curricular developments into other classrooms and schools.
2 Managing Teaching and Learning	Ensuring that every learner is inspired and challenged through an appropriate curriculum and a repertoire of teaching styles and skills that underpin personalized learning.	Development of a high degree of clarity about and consistency of teaching quality, both to create the regularities of practice that sustain improvement and to enable sharing of best practice and innovation across the system.
3 Developing people	Enabling students to become more active learners, develop thinking and learning skills and take greater responsibility for their own learning; involving parents and communities in this.	Development of schools as professional learning communities, with relationships built and fostered across and beyond schools to provide a range of learning experiences and professional development opportunities for staff.
4 Developing the organization	Creating an evidence-based school, with decisions informed effectively by student data, with self-evaluation and external support used to seek out approaches to school improvement that are appropriate to contextual needs and that build on other examples and practices.	Extending an organization's vision of learning to involve networks of schools collaborating to build, for instance, curriculum diversity, professional support, extended and welfare services and high expectations; in doing so, building a school's capacity to support wider system leadership roles.

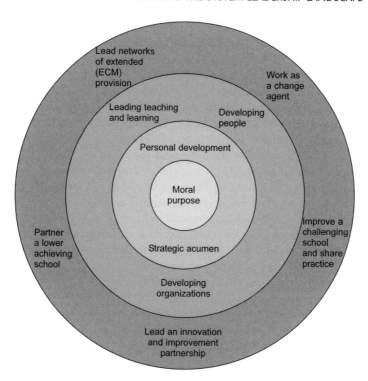

Figure 2.1 A model of system leadership practice

Finally, although there is a growing number of outstanding leaders that exemplify these qualities, they are not necessarily 'system leaders'. A system leader needs not only these aspirations and capabilities but also, as seen in the outer ring of the model, needs to work to change other contexts by engaging with the wider system in a meaningful way. We have included in the outer ring the range of roles identified from the research that focuses on: improving other schools, sharing curriculum innovations, empowering communities and/or leading partnerships committed to enabling all schools to move forward.

The model represents a powerful combination of practices that gives us a glimpse of leadership in a new educational landscape. Realizing that landscape, however, may also require a bigger shift within the broader education system.

Coda: the prospect for system leadership

This chapter has provided a conceptualization of system leadership and mapped the current landscape in England for the first time, using 2008 as a baseline. It has illustrated that there is already significant system leadership activity, more than previously expected. It has also demonstrated that system leadership can contribute decisively to a full range of government and local agendas by sharing expertise, facilities and resources in educational specialisms, innovation and creativity, leadership and management, vocational education and skills support. In addition, a full range of agendas for children's services and constructive links between parents and schools, businesses and further/higher education providers and schools are best served by such arrangements. The sharing of skills, expertise and experience creates much richer and more sustainable opportunities for rigorous transformation than can ever be provided by isolated institutions.

But we have also seen that the notion of system leadership itself is not unproblematic. There is evidence to show that replicating best practice from one school to others is not easily achieved. It is clear that there are limits to school leaders working across the system without becoming distracted from sustaining improvement in their own schools. There are also significant contradictions within, and tensions between, government-led system leadership and those increasing demands for giving school leaders more agency to take the lead. Above all, there has been a lack of evidence to demonstrate that school leaders engaged in system thinking and action can consistently provide solutions to complex systemic problems. This book intends to begin to fill that particular gap. For, while the whole idea of system-level reform is territory that is neither clearly charted nor uncontested, it is, as we have seen, beginning to be productively explored, in practice as well as theory, by the new breed of educational change adventurers. These are all issues we explore in detail in the subsequent five chapters.

3 Leadership of sustained improvement in challenging contexts

Headteachers of schools that have sustained their own improvement over a number of years, in our experience, are increasingly taking on roles that put their moral purpose and strategic intent to the task of improving the wider system. To take this step, and before system leaders fully engage externally, they first develop a deep and rigorous understanding of systems for improvement in their own schools. Without these core currencies of pedagogy, curriculum and student well-being, many would question whether they could lead improvements across the wider system. In this chapter we develop this argument about the link between school improvement and system leadership. We do so with reference to three in-depth case studies of schools serving disadvantaged urban areas.

The significance of these particular schools is twofold. First, with each having sustained improvement for about a decade, they are part of a small but increasing number of schools in challenging circumstances to have bucked the traditional trend towards low educational attainment and attendance and insufficient progression. We argue that, in having truly changed the contexts in which their staff teach and their students learn, these schools are contributing to system change: by providing an exemplar of how student outcomes can be improved; and by then sharing this intelligence with other schools locally. Having defined this work in the previous chapter as a specific system leadership role, we now explore in detail how such transformative improvement is being achieved in practice. We locate our argument in the broader school improvement tradition.

Second, and importantly for our argument here, each of the three schools is now taking on wider system roles. We are interested in why these schools have taken on other roles and what it is that each school brings to the task. In short, we provide a perspective on how other system leadership roles come about. The nascent literature in this area suggests that system roles demand capacity and readiness at various levels in a school, rather than simply heroic leadership ('super-heads'). We seek to advance and deepen this analysis by proposing a set of capabilities that these schools and leaders hold in common. Finally, it is confirmed that undertaking wider system roles on the one hand and sustaining school improvement on the other will probably become mutually reinforcing – with the caveat, particularly for schools in challenging circumstances, of an ongoing replenishment of internal capacity.

School improvement

From its roots in debates about whether 'schools make a difference' – relative to external socio-economic contextual factors and, in particular, the family – the literature on school improvement and school effectiveness has explored the internal components that characterize improving and/or effective schools. These components have been shown to include a positive 'ethos' (defined as the cumulative characteristics of values, attitudes and behaviours; Rutter et al. 1979), an emphasis on the curriculum and teaching (Purkey and Smith 1983) as well as shared vision and goals, high expectations and the monitoring of student progress (Sammons et al. 1995). Summarizing these school-level components and updating them from our contemporary research on school improvement, we propose nine key elements that need to be worked on at the same time. In no particular order, these are set out in Table 3.1.

Table 3.1   Components of an effective school

Teaching and learning	that is consistently good or better, with high expectations in the classroom, a shared 'good lesson' structure, a high proportion of time on task and use of assessment for learning to plan lessons and tailor tasks to individual needs.
Curriculum	that is balanced, interesting and active, with strategic planning to integrate core skills, breadth and cognitive learning, with interventions for catch-up and/or enrichment and mentoring.
Behaviour	that promotes order and enjoyment, with consistent rules for conduct and dress, and with consistently applied sanctions for infringement.
Attitudes to learning	that promote achievement, with high attendance, the celebration of success, accessible pastoral care and the voice of students valued in decision-making.
Leadership	with a clear vision that is translated into manageable, time-bound and agreed objectives, with commitment established and data used to tackle weaknesses and internal variation.
Learning community	with staff sharing experiences of improving practice, dedicated time for a range of CPD opportunities and a focus on identifying individual needs, especially where weak teaching exists.

Internal accountability	that 'empowers through a culture of discipline' rather than prescription, with agreed expectations for teaching, quality assurance and peer observation and the tracking of individual student achievement, attendance and behaviour.
Resource management	that is student-focused, with a creative use of funding streams, and workforce reform and an environment that supports learning and well-being.
Partnerships	beyond the school that create and extend learning opportunities, with parental engagement, and school-to-school collaborative work, and the support of external agencies focused on whole school priorities.

We may correctly postulate that a majority of reliable or high value-added schools will have these practices in place (or will be working towards any remaining). Such an approach to understanding school improvement, however, is open to two important criticisms. First, it can culminate, essentially, in a list so that little clue is given as to how each component is developed in practice. In this way, how an improvement trajectory is sustained or what challenges schools face along the way can remain underexplored. We often do not gain a perspective on how different components interact with each other as a part of a whole-school approach. How this interplay occurs will be constructed differently, of course, in each school. Our research suggests, however, that where this is a purposeful and coherent process and where staff are encouraged to engage in such 'systems thinking' (Senge 1990), the school is more likely to be able to diagnose its strengths and weakness and to work for improvements in teaching, learning and student outcomes. Where this interplay is absent or less developed, it appears more likely that a school's most effective work will be limited to several innovative departments.

The second criticism of the 'key components' approach is that it has paid too little attention to the external contexts that schools serve. This is the argument that challenging circumstances can hinder a school's ability to improve (Whitty 2001). The related objection is that the school improvement tradition has focused too heavily on generic practices that school staff should implement rather than on the specific challenges that they face in doing so (Thrupp 1999). Lupton (2005), for instance, argues that schools in more challenging contexts face above-average difficulties in staff recruitment and retention, significant pressures on teaching and management and a lack of resources, which reduce their capacity to respond to more complex social problems.

That multiple contextual disadvantages do, indeed, create additional challenges for schools seems irrefutable when one considers the impact of socio-economic background on student achievement. Feinstein et al.'s (2007) analysis of the 1970 British Cohort Study, for instance, shows significant inequalities in early cognitive development between socio-economic groups. School effectiveness studies have shown that social background factors explain over half the overall variation in pupil achievement (Reynolds et al. 2001). Our own analysis, set out in Figure 3.1, suggests, on average, that both the achievement of pupils eligible for free school meals (FSM) from 'hard pressed areas' is significantly below average in all schools, including in low deprivation schools and that contexts of high deprivation have a depressing impact on all students, including those from more wealthy backgrounds.

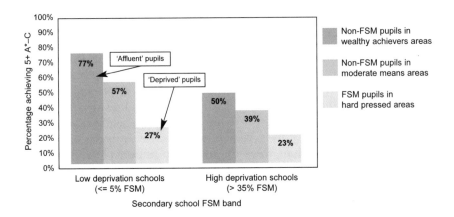

Figure 3.1 Student attainment, socio-economic background and school mix: the attainment of FSM and non-FSM pupils living in rich, moderate and poor areas and in low and high FSM schools

While we are still learning, as Levin (2006: 399) suggests, 'to understand how such contextual factors affect the work of school improvement', the literature is more advanced than its critiques allow. Gray et al. (1999), for instance, provided a range of case studies of improvement efforts and strategies in different contexts and at different 'stages of development'. More recently, Harris et al. (2006b: 412) have drawn on contingency theory to suggest that 'improving schools need to find a best fit between their internal conditions and the external contingency factors they are confronted with'.

In this chapter we seek to contribute to these debates. We analyse effective strategies for improvement in the face of social disadvantage. We provide a very detailed perspective on the processes of initiating, developing and sustaining a journey of improvement (rather than solely the components of an improved school). We then consider how this has led into, and enabled the schools to take on, wider system leadership roles.

To select schools that had sustained improvement over a long period, we sampled by GCSE, contextually value-added data and Ofsted judgements on the quality of leadership, teaching, welfare, and behaviour and attendance. Those in challenging circumstances were subsequently selected with reference to Ofsted's most recent description of each school, the percentage of students eligible for free school meals and qualitative intelligence. The research was undertaken in one whole-week research visit to each school. The research included semi-structured interviews with the headteacher, a group of governors, members of the senior management team (SMT), several middle leaders, and a number of teachers who had been at the school for a significant time. We also held group discussions with teachers and, separately, students, and we observed a number of lessons.

Sustaining improvement over the long term

Over a decade ago, both Robert Clack and Greenwood Dale had all the problems of very low achieving inner-city schools, including low expectations of and for students; a poor environment, with graffiti and dilapidated buildings; very poor behaviour, with little responsibility taken by senior leaders; a lack of direction and unity among staff; a significant financial deficit. Plashet School was in less visible crisis but had an ingrained culture of complacency. This underpinned teaching that was predominantly judged as only just satisfactory rather than good, a lack of challenge or differentiation for students, and few systems or shared practices that were organized for improvement.

All three schools continue to face very challenging circumstances. Robert Clack is a community, mixed comprehensive school and science college and serves an intake drawn from two of the most disadvantaged wards in the country. Greenwood Dale is a foundation, mixed comprehensive school and technology college. Unemployment in the inner-city area it serves is high and there is a range of socio-economic inequalities. Plashet is a community, comprehensive girls' school serving an urban area. Over half of its pupils are eligible for free school meals and the proportion of pupils for whom English is an additional language is over 90 per cent.

In the early 1990s, however, a new headteacher in each school provided a significant impetus for change, following their predecessors' retirement or early retirement. At Plashet, the successful candidate was a recently appointed new deputy head who told governors she wanted the school to be a place where she would send her own teenage children. At that time, she said, she would not because students were underachieving within a 'sympathy model' from which few with the potential went on to higher education. At Robert Clack the successful candidate was also promoted internally, from a head of department post. The local authority felt this was a significant risk, but the governors were convinced by both his vision for the school and the success of students within his history department which had consistently performed well above the school's average. At Greenwood Dale, the new headteacher was appointed from a deputy's post in another school. His clear and pragmatic vision for the school impressed parent governors who remember being desperate for stronger leadership for their school.

Following these appointments, that were made between 1992 (at Greenwood Dale) and 1996 (at Robert Clack) each school sustained improvement over a decade or more. Robert Clack increased for 11 consecutive years the percentage of students achieving at the GCSE benchmark, from 17 per cent in 1996 to 82 per cent now, with 50 per cent including English and mathematics. The school received a grade 1 in every category for consecutive Ofsted inspections in 2004 and 2007 (except for attendance in 2007). Greenwood Dale had narrowly escaped going into special measures during the early 1990s when 13 per cent of students achieved at the GCSE benchmark. Now 80 per cent do; 51 per cent with English and mathematics, and the school has a contextually valued-added (CVA) score of 1068. Plashet School now has 72 per cent of students achieving at the GCSE benchmark, 66 per cent with English and mathematics and a CVA score of 1019. These sustained improvements are demonstrated in terms of overall student attainment at GCSE in Figure 3.2.

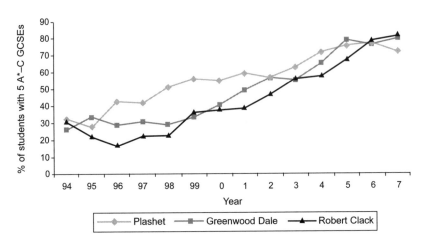

Figure 3.2 Student attainment at GCSE for the three schools since 1994

We turn now to what happened next during these improvement journeys. We are concerned with the contextual challenges faced by each school, the responses they developed, the improvement activities implemented and the leadership challenges in sustaining and evolving these activities. We find some significant similarities across the schools that coalesce around four main stages:

- narrative for improvement;
- organizing key improvement activities;
- putting professional learning at the heart of the process;
- changing dominant institutional cultures.

We consider each of these in turn, while also detailing the specific features of each school. There is some temporal sequencing, but also some overlap.

Narrative for improvement

Perhaps still clearest in the memory of staff present at the time is an initial phase in which each school laid the foundations for improvement. This included issues of behaviour, community engagement and teaching and learning. We focus here on three key elements to summarize these early actions.

First, in all three schools, the need for change was relatively plain. The challenge was to *translate a new mission into clear principles for action* and urgency for change. At Robert Clack, the new headteacher set out in his first week that 'this is going to be a very good school, serving the local community, focusing on success and building not just high aspirations for students, but high expectations of the school'. The principles for action were focused on ending abusive behaviour and creating a safe place to learn and work. This involved confronting a threatening minority of students and parents, writing new and clear school rules, permanently excluding a dozen seriously offending students and initiating pupil and parent contracts with the clear message that 'if you deviate from agreed rules, these are the consequences and they will be applied'. This was hard work that demanded a steely will from staff, leaders and, ultimately, the headteacher and governors to face up to aggression and demand that students change or leave. The school also worked to build a more positive external image since it was derided in the community. To alter this perception, the new leadership team worked to bring parents and the wider community into the new improvement project, including celebrating student successes at school events and in the local press. They also sought to manage the local community's experience of students' leaving time each day with senior leaders travelling on local buses, speaking to shopkeepers and taking action on poor behaviour where necessary.

Second, the need to *increase examination results and tackle weaknesses* in the quality of teaching was all too clear. At Greenwood Dale, the new leadership team was quick to act. Clear expectations were set out, 'can't do' attitudes were rejected and, in the first term, a curriculum and staff review was undertaken as part of the legal requirement related to redundancy procedures. This culminated in a quarter of the staff leaving the school in the first year and continued with half the school's middle leadership leaving over the next three years. Such a significant loss of staff could have created a demotivational effect for those that remained. However, staff present at the time remembered a realization that the new leadership team would stick by them and take personal responsibility for key challenges. This included teaching the lowest ability sets in core subjects as well as supervising all breaks and student transfers on the school's small site (practices that continue to date). Another strand was to tackle the inherited £200,000 budget deficit that resulted from student numbers falling to about 500. A reduction in staff was part of the strategy, but the leadership team also felt it needed full decision-making control over resources. This led to the school becoming grant maintained in 1993. In the longer term, the school reflects, this created a difficult relationship with the local authority, but this was balanced by the school developing, at an early stage, a freedom from external bureaucracy, a clear focus on its own priorities and the head's mantra that, 'If it is not statutory, we don't do it (unless we want to)'.

Third, *a clear reform narrative was developed* with work to ensure that this could be seen by a majority of staff to be consistently applied by the school leadership. At Plashet this meant a whole-school commitment to the eradication of the coasting culture and complacency. This was led by the new headteacher and two deputies who all taught and were reported by Ofsted to provide an excellent model for other teachers. Key appointments were made at middle manager level with the goal of moving from individual teacher to departmental schemes of work, appropriate textbooks and common assessment. Managed carefully and transparently, teachers responded with hard and effective work. Some reported overload, especially in terms of increased paperwork and accountability. But the majority remember feeling this was more than compensated for by the emerging evidence of a greater impact on student achievement. A culture of 'doing one's best' had started to develop and was being passed on to students. The school worked hard to change perceptions in their predominantly Muslim community in which too few parents had shown any initiative in their daughters' education. This included parental curricular evenings to discuss coursework and to communicate the principle that girls had a right to learn at home (rather than to be, often, Mum's helper). Undoubtedly, the role (model) of the new headteacher was highly significant here. She had become the first female Muslim headteacher in the country when she took over at Plashet. She visibly challenged the low traditional attainment of some minority ethnic groups and, in particular, British Pakistani and Bengali girls. She sought to communicate a message that combined an expectation for girls to compete and gain high core qualifications within a multi-cultural environment in which a range of religions would be openly discussed. Girls were encouraged to develop self-worth, both as part of a community but also through their own individuality.

Organizing the key improvement activities

Building on these foundations, each school increased student attainment in the first few years of the new headship. They all then entered a period in which student attainment remained static or, at least, increased significantly less rapidly. During this phase, the schools can be seen to have developed and implemented whole-school activities and systems that would sustain further improvement. We summarize these activities as three central themes.

First, there was *a whole-school focus on developing the quality of teaching and learning.* At each school the headteacher and members of the SMT told us that staff had expressed concerns that context and the background of students rendered the school's expectations for student learning and exam results unrealistic. The unanimous response of SMTs was that they would work to remove any barriers to teaching and learning that staff identified but, in return, they would expect, as one put it, 'quality teaching delivered regularly by motivated teachers with well planned lessons'. At Robert Clack, this focus included the school's 'good lesson guide'. This was based on the head-teacher's and key colleagues' diagnosis of best practice in the school, com-bined with an analysis of Mortimore's (1998) principles for improvement. At its heart, the guide echoed the National Strategies' priority for clear learning objectives, differentiation and a plenary. Associated teaching skills were dis-cussed in twilight in-service meetings and all new staff went (and still go) on induction weekends. Relatedly, teaching quality was regularly reviewed by the SMT through lesson observation and the monitoring of student work to ensure a whole-school focus. The SMT reported that teachers who were having difficulties were given extra support, but this was and remains a tricky balance to strike. Indeed, some staff felt that the weight of such account-ability made them wary of admitting weaknesses for fear of the intensity of the subsequent response from the leadership. It was thus vital to this approach that middle leaders bought into the internal accountability system, and worked for it, upholding a consistent message with the SMT. This was frequently achieved by heads of department at Robert Clack who acknowl-edged the pressure, but said they motivated staff by keeping focused on improving the value-added data and by explaining increased achievement in terms of improved classroom delivery.

Second, *improvement activities were regularly reviewed, evaluated and rede-veloped if necessary.* At Greenwood Dale, this was vital. Following the introduction of whole-school strategies to increase examination results (including a focus on borderline students), the percentage of students achieving at the GCSE benchmark increased from 13 per cent in 1992 to 27 per cent two years later. Following this initial success, this measure of school improvement plateaued at around 30 per cent for the next four years. Of course, as Elmore (2004) argues, plateaux can be entirely expected, with gains in performance being followed by a period in which teachers consolidate new skills and identify the next barriers. This appears to have happened at Greenwood Dale. A number of ways of working, that subsequently helped the school move off the plateau, were being developed and institutionalized. The school looked to build the cumulative effect of consistently doing several key things well. In a context of fragility, this included whole-school regularities in roles, teaching, marking, behaviour and support. These were codified in the staff handbook and supported by in-service training so that all staff knew what they were being asked to do and how this fitted together within the school's strategic plan. Some might have said that they were 'over-managed', but this enabled the SMT to decide on priorities and ensure everyone knew what was expected. A substantial commitment was also made to curriculum development within a wider debate about what worked best for the school's context. The focus was on developing exciting schemes of work to engage and motivate pupils better. This included, in the mid-1990s, the combination of English with media studies to provide, alongside key texts, a wide range of film, TV, journalism and, more recently, internet resources.

Third, there was *the development of highly reliable school systems and clear leadership roles* that supported improvement activities. At each school, the focus on improving student outcomes was supported by an internal accountability system. At Plashet, at the start of the academic year, each head of department was expected to provide a detailed report on outcomes (by teacher, set and social factors) to the SMT. This would lead into analysis, for instance, that in the mathematics department there was a need to target lower achievers in Key Stage 3 because, while progression from level 4 to 5 and from 5 to 6 was good, progression from level 3 to level 4/5 was below the national average. Targets for the following year would then be set. Progression throughout the year was monitored by a tracking system (initially for every class, and now for every student). Students were tested every half term, data were recorded in a standard record sheet and the heads of department were responsible for identifying (a lack of) progress against individual targets. From a culture of complacency, where a lack of progress might have been explained away (with reference to text books, a lack of support or the students them-selves), these changes represented a very different approach and some tea-chers reported feeling a lack of trust and 'very accountable'. But, supported by clear data for challenging practice, a willingness to back up targeted change with resources and with the principle of 'no blame, but concern if there is an emerging pattern', the school leadership sought to create a culture of openness where difficult staffing issues were responded to professionally.

Professional learning at the heart of the process

Permeating these activities and their organization, a third set of strategic practices focused on professional learning within the improvement process. In part, this happened within the work already described, especially where, as in the first example below, professional learning was needed for the implementation of new practice. This also developed, however, so that professional learning came reciprocally to inform practice and contribute to furthering the improvement process – as in the second and third examples below.

First, *the improvement strategy identified professional development needs*. At Robert Clack, running parallel to the school's 'good lesson' guide, twilight in-service training focused on what an outstanding lesson looked like and how this could be combined with new ideas about how pupils learn effectively. This led into on-the-job learning. Teachers were given opportunities to diagnose peer strengths and weaknesses through informal lesson observation (using Ofsted criteria). Middle leaders were coached in leading teaching, learning and curriculum organization and development. The SMT portfolios moved round periodically so that members came to know what each role demanded and the school gained the related professional development and capacity-building benefits. Distributed leadership thus became an increasing feature of professional development, but with the caveat that responsibility was distributed only when the SMT felt sufficient capability was in place.

Second, there was *the emergence of innovation*. As the schools institutionalized new minimum standards and systems across a majority of departments, many had already started to innovate. This was not normally innovation that produced radically new or alternative solutions. It was predominantly practical and incremental in nature. Indeed, as members of each SMT acknowledged, the schools would not even now be at the very vanguard of individual advances in, for instance, ICT or workforce reform, but they would be solidly placed in many developments and would be proficient at exploiting the links between them. At Greenwood Dale, in response to the very low and variable prior attainment of its students that came from 23 different primary schools, a Year 7 base was built and staffed by a strong mix of experienced and innovative teachers. This underpinned the provision of a common teaching approach to reading, knowledge and skills in Year 7 and the ability to instill the school's particular ethos of behaviour and expectations. The school also committed £280,000 per annum to support literacy in primary schools and student transition. The guiding innovation was to develop transition and Year 7 provision that could be increasingly responsive to individual students' learning needs. Professional learning was also placed at the heart of externally driven curriculum development. Both the National Literacy and Key Stage 3 Strategies were implemented at Greenwood Dale, but only after a significant rethink by all teachers to take key changes on board while keeping their own established good practice. This developed a culture of rigorously analysing what worked best and then sharing this with colleagues, both informally and, more recently, within best practice seminars organized by a deputy head to be short sharp inputs of 'radical and effective' practice that could then be followed up internally. This was supported by the early introduction of ICT, so that now departmental schemes of work are available to all staff on their own networked computers.

Third, *effective practice is increasingly shared internally*. This was perhaps most developed at Plashet. It commenced with the SMT working to transform what had become cumbersome, departmental and administrative in-service training so as to make it more responsive both to staff needs and the school improvement plan. This was combined with an opening up of more debate about external practice, with those attending external CPD events 'cascading' feedback on their return and with the SMT organizing whole-school workshops on particularly interesting and relevant external courses. Over time, the school became an 'increasingly safe' place to share practice, with a majority of staff willing to run in-service and peer training and to work with others outside their own department to jointly improve teaching strategies. The co-construction of practice also became a key focus of professional development within departments. For instance, the science department challenged itself to make learning more fun. To do so, the team researched and bought new resources and activities, integrated these into their existing schemes of work to ensure pace and differentiation, hired an IT consultant to put the outcomes together onto the school network, and then observed and coached each other across a range of key lessons. This was supported by timetabled planning meetings for each department every week. While, initially, this had been focused on administration, there was always now an agenda item on new skills, equipment, and so on. The headteacher saw that collaborative professional development had played an important role in improving the quality of teaching and learning which, as set out in Table 3.2, has been clearly demonstrated by Ofsted's inspections.[1]

Table 3.2 Ofsted judgements on the quality of observed teaching at Plashet over three inspections between 1993 and 2005

	1993	1999	2005
% of teaching satisfactory	88	97	99
% good or better	42.4	73	80

Institutional cultures are changed

The fourth and final set of improvement practices we identified concerned how values and an ethos that supported effective learning and professional development were established in the schools. These included the following.

First, *positive attitudes to learning*. At Robert Clack, teachers commented that the 'culture had changed, from about 50 per cent of students wanting to learn to over 90 per cent'. As we have seen, consistent discipline was crucial, with all staff expected to undertake roles in reinforcing calm and with high pupil awareness of what was (un)acceptable. But, over time, this was subtly married to a culture of listening to students and trying to understand perceived injustice, emphasizing praise for social responsibility as well as achievement, and underpinning this with a staff ethos that: 'If you give students respect, you get it back from them'. At Plashet, where there had originally been less disruptive behaviour, staff reported a slightly different transformation in learning attitudes: from a majority of quite sheltered girls who learnt passively to much greater student confidence with more willingness to take chances and be imaginative in the classroom. This also fed into an expectation by students for progression to college, with about 98 per cent now doing so. In all three schools, however, the achievement of high value-added outcomes could also be connected with some teachers feeling that they had to 'spoon-feed' students. There was the sense that they did not instil a full range of independent learning skills and experiences that would enable students to fully access the wider curriculum (and lifelong learning). In part, staff explained this as resulting from wanting the best for students, providing them with a wide range of resources, stimuli and support, and students coming to expect this and not thinking sufficiently for themselves. A number of staff suggested that, if they did not work in these ways, they would be worried about the impact on student attainment, especially in coursework, and the consequences for their own accountability.

Second, *a culture of professional action* reduced the need for excessive managerial pressure and control. Pressure remained, but the need for senior leadership intervention decreased. At Plashet, for instance, the school is now open from 8am till 5pm every day and on Saturday mornings for clubs, booster classes, and extra-curricular activities. As teachers reported, 'If the kids ask, the school will try' and the SMT will always explore opportunities to support these activities creatively with resources. To provide these activities as well as high quality lessons, teachers in all three schools felt that they worked very hard, and often harder than colleagues in other schools. Successive good Ofsted inspections and good appointments had developed a stable staff, high morale and healthy competition in the professional pursuit of excellence. This was supported by good school development planning, with a focus on students and based on a deep and wide consultation with teachers, governors, parents and students on the strengths to hold on to and the weakness to resolve. Each school also surveyed the forthcoming local and national policy landscape with openness to new ideas but a rigorous analysis of the evidence and implications for practice. In doing so, the schools have developed the confidence to define what they wanted to do and to filter external initiatives, aligning those that were important to internal priorities. As professional communities, each school had learnt to reproduce what it knew to be important to its own success.

Wider system roles

These cases provide a rich seam of evidence of how schools work in challenging circumstances to sustain improvement. While contextually different, a high degree of similarity existed. As significantly, each school has also continued its improvement journey by taking on wider system roles *that share their knowledge and practice with other schools*. Indeed, this finding is all the more striking given that no criterion on 'undertaking a wider system role' was included in the sampling process. To explore these emerging roles and the challenges they bring, we turn to the experiences of the three schools, before considering the broader themes to which these point.

At Robert Clack, over time, the school's clear focus on engaging the local community in its improvement developed into a wider role beyond the school. In 2004, Robert Clack's headteacher took on an ad-hoc consultant leader role to a neighbouring school. This began when the local authority contacted Robert Clack in the July to ask how it could help improve a local school that had gone into special measures, lost its headteacher and was unable to recruit a replacement. The model Robert Clack's headteacher proposed was to support an acting headteacher promoted from within. The rationale was that, led by an acting head, and hence supported rather than 'taken over' by another school, the local school's staff and leadership would be more deeply involved (and motivated) in developing its own capacity to improve.

It was a big commitment. Detailed plans for the following term were developed during August. These included:

- diagnosis of the key practices the neighbouring school needed to develop;
- clarity on Robert Clack's teaching and learning and behaviour systems;
- a visit to Robert Clack for 30 of the school's staff in September to witness the behaviour management, assemblies, and teaching and learning in action;

- the export to and refining of key systems into the partner school, employing key Robert Clack staff to deliver, in particular, Ofsted's requirements for immediate improvements in behaviour.

A pattern of two days a week consultant leadership by Robert Clack's head then developed. This included hands-on support for the implementation of the behaviour system. The outcome was that, at the first special measures monitoring inspection the following January (2005), Ofsted affirmed significant progress had been made. In Ofsted's judgement, the presence of a consultant and other senior leaders attesting to improvement and demonstrating continued commitment was important. After this success, and in agreement with the local authority, the acting headteacher was handed overall responsibility. The consultant role reduced to one of advice. Later that year the school came out of special measures and, subsequently, appointed a new headteacher.

There were also benefits to Robert Clack, as the 'lead' school, including:

- confidence for the leadership to know what needed to be done to get another school out of special measures;
- a contribution from staff both to help another school through a situation many had faced themselves and to gain unique leadership development;
- the overall experience which led into Robert Clack's current roles as a mentor school for the London Challenge and as a lead school in an SSAT network.

The flip-side was that Robert Clack needed to be willing to put the school's resources to the test. Indeed, with hindsight, Robert Clack's head acknowledges that he was fortunate to have had key logistics in place before taking on a wider improvement role. These included being in a local situation in which everyone, from the local authority, the partner school's governors and staff, and the wider community, was committed to the same key outcomes. The experience has given the leadership a clearer sense of Robert Clack's potential to undertake further system leadership. They evaluate that the headteacher has the capacity to advise and, from time to time, make strategic visits, which could be supported by several experienced teachers, to transfer and refine best practice. But to sustain Robert Clack's own improvement the school would need to be resourced to backfill.

Issues of capacity were also evident at Plashet. The school's well developed systems and its culture of sharing best practice internally provided strong foundations for the school to take on wider system roles. Its actual moves to do so also reflected a deeply ingrained and deliberate planning culture. The SMT took two years to consider how to continue to raise achievement while, at the same time, taking on wider local system roles. The leadership was clear it would neither put Plashet under pressure nor act before bringing a majority of staff on board. There were several steps.

First, in 2002, Plashet became a Beacon school with four themes of: leadership and management; gifted and talented provision; special educational needs; and extra-curricular provision. Each theme was led by a head of department responsible for organizing all interaction with other schools. Initially, a number of staff expressed concern about an increase in workload and a decrease in results. They were given assurances by the SMT that, if Beacon status produced either, the school would come out of the programme. A review at re-designation showed staff had been paid for extra time, results had gone up and a range of staff had gained significant professional development. More qualitatively, there was a growing confidence to analyse and share practice with colleagues. At first, there had been a common belief that 'the school was good because of the girls, and thus how could teachers share practice with schools that had poor behaviour and less committed students'. Beacon status developed processes of self-evaluation to enhance skills in identifying and sharing more effective practice.

In 2004, Plashet became a Leading Edge school with three themes: leadership and management; provision for gifted and talented students; and a school ethos to promote high achievement from low prior attainment. Building on Beacon status, Plashet developed as a 'lead' school. Many departments developed the capacity to work externally and a number could identify that their wider work and output came back to Plashet as expertise in the longer term. A key principle remained – that of also maintaining the school's capacity in the shorter term. To do so, Plashet kept half of the £40,000 it then received as a Leading Edge school. After covering travel and supply costs, the residue was made available for curriculum development.

Finally, the school's development of wider roles led to the headteacher becoming a SIP in 2005. A number of key issues had already emerged. First, Plashet's headteacher found it essential to have her own school ready to act as a 'lead'. For example, following SIP discussions concerning underperformance in another school's science department, she offered a visit to her own highly improved department. The visiting headteacher and head of department discussed and viewed with Plashet's science staff the online curriculum, schemes of work and teaching resources, as well as observing Plashet's approach to active teaching and learning in the classroom. This direct and ongoing sharing of best practice was considered invaluable. It also enabled Plashet's headteacher to focus on sharing what works within a SIP model of support and challenge rather than being cast as an inspector. For her, this differentiation was crucial to her success. Second, there was again a focus on maintaining capacity at Plashet, with the SIP resources being used to upgrade several SMT members who took on additional roles within the school. While this was secure, Plashet's headteacher did have concerns for the growing role of acting as a SIP in relation to both the National Strategies and Ofsted reports. Since she was a SIP of three schools, with formal and informal responsibilities, the local authority wanted a commitment of 13 days for each school. This, she considered, was a maximum.

Experiences of wider system roles at Greenwood Dale started when the headteacher was seconded for a year to Serco Education (then Quality Assurance Associates) to work as Head of School Improvement in Walsall Education. Having returned to Greenwood Dale, this led into several local roles to support lower achieving schools. In each case, it was the headteacher who agreed to take responsibility for providing support but it was one of the deputy heads who led the project on a day-to-day basis. The first was River Leen school where, during 2006/07, Greenwood Dale worked to help develop a number of improvement strategies including in mathematics, whole school tracking and targeting of student progress and support for Year 11 students. One Greenwood Dale deputy head spent four days a week at River Leen, two assistant heads worked there part time, other staff provided support when needed and River Leen staff were mentored by their peers at Greenwood Dale. River Leen improved from 23 per cent of students gaining 5 A*–C grades in 2006 to 41 per cent in 2007.

The second school was Elliot Durham, a close neighbour of Greenwood Dale, that serves a community facing severe social and economic disadvantage and with students entering with exceptionally low prior attainment (according to Ofsted's inspection in 2007). It is a small school of just 430 students with falling rolls. Since 1998, student achievement at GCSE hovered around 10 per cent gaining 5 A*–C grades and more recently it had had a number of changes in leadership. At the local authority's request Greenwood Dale supported the acting headteacher in particular to help the school avoid going into 'special measures'. Five weeks later, Elliot Durham was deemed 'satisfactory' by Ofsted and the partnership support recognized in the inspection report. Another of Greenwood Dale's deputy heads, having worked with the acting headteacher as an associate head during this time, took over himself as acting head in 2007/08. Greenwood Dale's headteacher acted as the informal executive head of the two schools. This was formalized when, as part of the first cohort in 2007, he became a National Leader of Education and Greenwood Dale a National Support School.

Plans for a more formal support partnership had existed from before receiving NLE status. This was initially for a hard support federation. However, as detailed project planning developed and discussions were held with local and national government, the concept of a 3–18 Academy started to emerge, with the willing inclusion of a local primary school. By September 2008 this proposal had been backed by the city council. The Academy will have three sites with, respectively, 3–15 provision, 11–18 provision and 15/16–18 provision. With a projected total of 3520 children it will become the biggest school in England. It will also become the first Academy to be sponsored by a state school, in this case by Greenwood Dale. A local employer, Experian, will become the business supporter and bring experience of building projects and IT infrastructure. Greenwood Dale has raised £60 million for rebuilding the sites and redesigning the educational offer. Central government has pledged £45m to pay for the secondary dimension, with the City Council providing £10.5m for the primary site.

The whole Academy will be led by one executive leader – likely to be Greenwood Dale's current headteacher – who, with a central team, will oversee standards, finance and personnel. Three heads of school – likely to be the two Greenwood Dale deputies and the existing primary headteacher – will take responsibility for the day-to-day running of each site. This 'schools within a school' model is designed to ensure pupils are taught in smaller units rather than in one very large organization. The proposed opening dates for the new Academy will be September 2009 (in existing buildings) and 2011 in new or refurbished buildings on each site.

Coda: institutional capabilities

Continuing to sustain school improvement on the one hand and undertake wider system roles on the other does appear to be potentially reinforcing. The important caveat is that this necessitates sufficient whole-school and leadership capacity. Hence, whereas in the subsequent chapters we go on to explore how wider system roles have been taken on more fully, we have demonstrated here that schools, and particularly those in challenging circumstances, will as a priority want to remain vigilant about sustaining their own school's improvement. Equally, we have also seen that sustaining improvement can help to develop the skills and capacities required for wider system roles, even in challenging circumstances. This is an important finding as it tests the thesis that system leadership can extend from schools serving disadvantaged communities. The counter argument that system leadership is an elite activity serving the financial and professional interests of schools in leafy suburbs – that will inevitably (re)produce a two tier education system – appears unfounded. While we are attentive to reproducing such inequalities, the argument does not do justice to the work of schools like Robert Clack, Greenwood Dale and Plashet.

In seeking to capture these findings conceptually, and by way of concluding this chapter, we propose below a set of five hypotheses about (what might best be called) the *institutional and leadership capabilities* that these schools brought to the task of their emerging system leadership roles. The purpose here is to hypothesize how school improvement journeys can aid and contribute to a school's ability to take on wider system roles.

First, as we have seen, the leadership teams explicitly organized their schools for improvement. They did so by providing a clear reform narrative, seen by a majority of staff to be consistently applied, and by strategically linking together whole-school improvement activities that were supported by clear leadership roles. A key leadership challenge was that, after improvement gains, plateaux in performance could be expected. Leaders needed to ensure complacency did not set in and encourage teachers to consolidate new skills and identify the next barriers to progress. In this way, the first hypothesis to emerge is the ability of system leaders to *determine the capacity needed to undertake other improvement activities*. This includes intelligence about what is important for success, associated skills of planning, implementing and monitoring change, and the leadership acumen to ensure that one's own capacity to deliver core day-to-day tasks is not undermined.

Second, as one deputy head argued, the schools created clarity (of key whole-school systems they established), consistency (as these systems spread across the school), and continuity (of the systems over time). A key challenge for the schools was that, while they had succeeded in the face of significant socio-economic challenge, they remained constantly aware of their fragility, given the contexts they served (especially at Robert Clack and Greenwood Dale). Clear systems had been developed and refined over time, a very high percentage of staff knew and implemented their responsibilities and each school's leaders provided a visible presence in tackling key issues. The second hypothesis this develops for wider roles is the importance of *understanding the regularities needed to sustain improvement in a school* and the ability to decide on and deliver priorities.

Third, the leadership in each school was focused on improving the quality of teaching, learning and student well-being to ensure every learner became inspired and challenged to achieve and also to reduce identified barriers to achievement. To do so, the schools had gone some way to balancing the development of literacy and numeracy skills for all students with a broader curricular offer and differentiation in the classroom. Sometimes the achievement of high value-added outcomes had been connected with teachers feeling that they had to 'spoon-feed' students. This was an ongoing professional challenge, as teachers worked hard in the pursuit of both high achieving and well-rounded young people. The third hypothesis is that wider system roles were aided by an already *ingrained ethos of high expectations* for students and of teachers, so that institutional values supported professional development and a culture of motivation and goodwill among staff. This was vital to sustain the 'beyond the call of duty working' that appeared to be necessary to achieve long-term improvement and to taking on wider system roles.

Fourth, internal accountability was a feature of each school. As a consequence, some staff 'felt very accountable' and, in a few cases, reported negative effects where pressure for student attainment had led teachers to be less creative in teaching and curriculum planning. However, over time and where successfully implemented, most crucially by middle leaders, the schools had nurtured, to different degrees, a dominant culture where professional action reduced the need for excessive managerial pressure. In particular, regular peer observation and collaborative planning helped to create a shared language about what was being found effective in engaging students in their learning. The fourth hypothesis is the importance of a widely developed ability to *identify and transfer or co-construct practice* internally that, in turn, provides the potential for schools to work externally to share systems, skills and experience with other colleagues.

Fifth, and importantly for our concerns at the start of this chapter for the impact of socio-economic context on school improvement, the leadership of all three schools shared an aspiration to 'change context' as a key component of their improvement strategies. To do so, and as we have seen, they looked outwards to developed educational strategies that were explicitly responsive to their localities, to engage parents and the wider community in the improvement project and to build partnerships for high aspirations and student well-being outside the school's gates (a theme we substantially develop in the next chapter). This was challenging and time-consuming. Yet, our case study schools all showed significant changes that they had led in partnership with their communities. So, the fifth hypothesis is that this provides the necessary experience of *working, negotiating and building networks of stakeholders*, including local schools, parent bodies and governors, as well as local authorities and national agencies, that are all essential to sustaining improvements in student attainment and well-being.

4 Leading innovation and improvement partnerships: the case of Leading Edge

A hypothesis that has long held appeal is that there are solutions elsewhere in the education system for challenges faced in individual schools. The trouble is, we have not always known where these solutions are or how best to apply them to other contexts. Recent advances may have made this a more realistic aim to fulfil. Since the mid-1990s, teachers have become increasingly willing and/or expected to be observed, to observe others and to discuss their pedagogic practice. Schools commonly use comparative data in their own self-evaluation. A wide range of local partnerships and national networks bring teachers and school leaders together to innovate and share ideas. We may also be finding out how schools are doing this. Approaches under the banner of 'knowledge transfer', for instance, have not always been found appropriate in collaborative settings. Schools working together collegially may also be 'co-constructing' new practices to common challenges (Fielding et al. 2005).

As part of this emerging national context, this chapter explores the leadership of innovation and improvement partnerships. In Chapter 2 we defined these as being two or more schools working on specific themes of mutual interest or challenge. We also suggested that leading an effective innovation partnership constitutes a system leadership role. To consider these arguments in practice, we focus here on Leading Edge partnerships as a case study for our analysis. The chapter progresses in four main ways. First, it describes the Leading Edge Partnership Programme and exemplifies the work of local partnerships through a specific case study. Second, it explores the main themes and impacts of Leading Edge partnership work. We find both a focus on innovating personalized learning strategies and an emerging set of positive impacts that emanate from their implementation. Most clearly the impacts are for a number of groups of students, collaborating professionals and several low-achieving schools. Third, the chapter considers the methodologies of collaborative innovation. We find a number of effective working practices, but also propose a model of how schools might work together with greater rigour. Fourth, the chapter analyses the skills and tasks that appear to be implicated in the system leadership of effective innovation partnerships. These include approaches to capacity-building, developing leaders at a range of levels, lateral accountability to sustain progress, and a partnership vision and ethos that support mutual improvement.

Leading Edge

The concept of a 'leading edge' reflects a government aspiration to encourage schools to innovate collaboratively and share practices that 'tackle some of the most intractable barriers to raising standards' (DCSF website, accessed 10 February 2008). The resultant Leading Edge Partnership Programme (LEPP) was launched in 2003. It was a successor to the Beacon Schools Programme that had existed since 1998. The initial programme had funded high-achieving schools to disseminate aspects of their practice to other schools, but usually without any sustained support or interaction. The Leading Edge Partnership Programme sought to learn from the limitations of this approach by demanding a more clearly defined local partnership in which a 'lead' school and several 'partner' schools could work together.

The Leading Edge Partnership Programme now connects about 200 lead schools with about 800 partners. Lead schools receive around £60,000 per annum on behalf of their partnership. It is intended that these funds are used to support both innovation and the raising of standards in partner schools. When spread across an average partnership size of four or five schools, this does not constitute a large contribution to school budgets. However, it does enable school leaders to seed new projects, backfill staff working out of school within the timetable, and/or to take on coordination and other partnership costs. With 212 partnerships, covering about a third of secondary schools in England, LEPP also represents a relatively significant systemic commitment.

In 2006, the central leadership of the programme was migrated out of central government (and specifically the Innovation Unit) to the SSAT. The Innovation Unit had, unusually for government, allowed schools to develop projects organically without much guidance or any clear accountability for their use of funds. The SSAT sought to combine this initial mandate with slightly more accountability for partnership progress and a clearer central offer, including national conferences, workshops, online tools and visits by partnership leaders.

While we refer to the support and challenge provided by this national programme, our focus is on the leadership and work undertaken in and across local partnerships themselves. To exemplify this work we first consider the case study of Oldham.

Oldham

There are two Leading Edge partnerships in Oldham. One contains four schools, another five, but there is some overlap. Many of the schools serve challenging contexts in a metropolitan borough challenged by segregation and deprivation. This was highlighted by riots in 2001 that reportedly involved many young men from minority ethnic groups. Social segregation is notable in education, with several schools serving either 90 per cent British Bangladeshi, Pakistani or White students. The schools, however, have built strong collaborative links. There is a protocol to share student attainment data and identify strengths and weaknesses across all the secondary schools in Oldham. This current work sustains earlier developments under the Leadership Incentive Grant, so that now all schools allocate 10 per cent of their deprivation funding to finance a local authority data group. They also fund two of their own headteachers as local consultant heads to mentor other leadership teams and contribute to local strategic planning.

The first Leading Edge partnership focuses on a 'traffic light' student tracking system, available in real time to all staff. This was developed in the lead school and shared with partner schools who, in turn, aided its development. The system can now analyse attainment data by department, class, pupil, postcode and targeted group. The partner schools say this has been very beneficial. For instance, one saw the partnership as a direct contribution to its progress from 16 per cent of students in 2004 gaining 5 A*–C grades at GCSE to 41 per cent in 2007, with attendance rates also increasing from 83 per cent to 92 per cent. This work was recognized by Ofsted in 2007 which reported that 'one of the school's strengths, and a significant factor in its on-going improvement, is the willingness to share good practice and to learn from others'. Ofsted also alluded, however, to the difficulties of transferring practice. It detailed how, 'although the school makes use of assessment, some of it is unreliable and systems for collation are not consistent'. The implication is that student tracking needs to be combined with professional development, a point recognized by the headteacher who is working with middle leaders to improve formative assessment and the interpretation of data.

The second partnership focused initially on tackling underachievement among boys. Target groups were identified in each school with 15 boys in Years 8 and 10 who were unlikely, on current evidence, to fulfil their potential at GCSE. Motivational strategies were developed, including use of music technology and aspirational visits linked to attendance at booster classes. Several schools experimented with teaching strategies with one, for instance, working to help move boys from subject understanding to written explanation. After two years there was some significant progress. All the target Year 10 boys in one school achieved five A*–Cs and, overall, boys' achievement in the partnership increased over the project. On reflection, however, the schools felt they were not sufficiently clear on what had been successful in each other's institutions, in part as there had been little collaborative observation.

A second phase has recently refocused on mathematics. The impetus came not only from new government accountability targets but also from the headteachers' review of CVA data for mathematics which showed only one school in the partnership to be above the national average. It was felt that the departments could benefit from joint development of curriculum resources and pedagogy. The heads of mathematics departments were brought together, under the leadership of the lead school's headteacher, and it was agreed to share existing practice, jointly plan new teaching resources and implement these in each school with scheduled time for cross-partnership observation and evaluation. This is a demanding agenda that will require good relationships and trust between teachers and skilful collaborative leadership by headteachers to sustain one another's full engagement in Leading Edge activity.

Oldham was one of five case study partnerships we researched. These were selected to represent different social, economic and regional contexts and to span a range of partnership sizes and length of engagement in LEPP. The research included two-day visits across each partnership. This engagement comprised: at the lead school, interviews with the headteacher and at least five members of staff involved in partnership work; at two partner schools, interviews with the headteacher, a head of department and a teacher. Where possible, a collaborative activity was also observed. To test the wider generalizability of the findings, an early draft of this chapter was presented to a workshop of about forty school leaders at the 2007 LEPP annual conference in both York and London.

Collaborative advantage

The five Leading Edge partnerships were engaged in a wide range of work. There were also several important similarities. These included:

- a collaborative ethos, with the majority of lead and partner schools reporting positively on each other's commitment to partnership working and their own willingness to contribute to the partnership's development;
- evidence of trust, with at least two-thirds of the partnerships demonstrating among a majority of schools a relatively high level of trust in one another to deliver their strategic and/or operational responsibilities;
- a history to partnership membership, with previous collaborative work often having taken place between a number of the schools, and

the explicit inclusion of one or more historically lower-achieving schools serving challenging circumstances;

- a co-existence of the Leading Edge partnership with a range of other collaboratives that were emerging or ongoing, but that did not necessarily include all of the LEPP partnership members.

There were also a range of clearly identifiable positive impacts for professionals from Leading Edge work, in many of the schools, in the majority of the partnerships. In increasing degrees of collaborative depth, these can be summarized as:

- improved professional support, with the majority of teachers reporting the benefits of an extended network of curricular-relevant assistance, and heads of department finding a means to overcome isolation, particularly when having been given the task of boosting the results of a low-achieving department;
- increased opportunities to gain inspiration and pool ideas for practice with colleagues in an informal setting and based on professional dialogue and judgement;
- high quality professional development in the workplace with the opportunity to generate wider professional learning communities among staff, and support and coaching for leaders at a variety of levels;
- the collaborative development of new practice, with not only the transfer or refinement of what was already perceived to be good practice but also the joint identification of challenges and then the research and innovation of responsive teaching techniques, resources and/or wider learning opportunities.

These positive impacts and similarities correspond well with the wider research literature that points to commitment, trust, support, professional development and time for collaborative inquiry as key elements of effective partnership working (Reynolds 2004; Rudd et al. 2004; Spender 2006; Arnold 2006) and the creation of 'collaborative advantage' (Huxham and Vangen 2005).

There was also evidence of a LEPP impact on student outcomes. Two forms were most common. The first concerned a contribution to *whole school improvement in a partner school* (or schools) that had previously been underachieving, often in challenging circumstances. Across the five partnerships and since the start of their Leading Edge work, two schools had improved out of special measures, one from a notice to improve and two from low achievement. The key strategies stemming from LEPP work that the schools reported to have been significant in improvement included:

- student tracking and assessment for learning (in the majority);
- wider curriculum pathways;
- leadership support and mentoring;
- motivation and support (for students at risk);
- approaches to challenging low expectations, including through developing a new culture of inquiry – at least among a cadre of teachers.

The second common impact concerned improved attainment, behaviour, attendance and/or engagement by *students in a target group*. In these instances the strategies reported to be most successful included students:

- targeted due to under-performance;
- supported and mentored in small groups or as a part of an extended student welfare strategy;
- re-engaged by new curriculum pathways;
- aided during transition to secondary school.

There were some important caveats to this. Identifiable progress was rarely partnership-wide, with usually only some schools moving forward. Where progress had occurred, Leading Edge work was often a contributing factor but it would have been difficult to demonstrate its proportional impact. The schools themselves recognized this. Where a specific group of students had been targeted, it was rare for all of them to have moved forward, with (more usually) progress for a majority but less impact for a minority. There was also a range of work for which no improvement in student attainment could be demonstrated. Perhaps the most important reason for this was that the partnerships had initially viewed LEPP as not being bound to the strictures of short-term increases in standards. They had, therefore, included longer-term challenges or objectives more amenable to professional judgement rather than those judged solely by increases in student attainment (at least in the short term).

Leading Edge partnerships, however, were working to develop a range of innovative practice that sought to respond better to the needs, interests and potential of their students. In one form or another, this was the major focus of their partnership. In analysing this work, we focus first on the strategies developed to personalize learning. We then consider the collaborative methodologies employed to do so, before turning to how school leaders responded to the challenges of leading an innovation partnership.

Strategies for personalizing learning

The innovative practice that had been developed by the five case study partnerships coalesced around five key categories. These were as follows.

First, the development of new *teaching and learning strategies*, often undertaken in response to an identified whole-school weakness or as part of a departmental improvement plan. These included:

- developing the use of ICT as a support for teaching, with innovation in the use of whiteboards and electronic voting, and to support the extension of learning beyond the classroom. This included learning materials being accessed through virtual learning environments (VLEs) for catch-up, for gifted and talented students, parental involvement and revision;
- challenging low expectations with, for instance, secondary staff observing primary classes as part of an approach to overcoming an identified dip in Year 7. A common finding was that high levels of pace and challenge in Year 6 were lacking in Year 7.

Second, *assessment for learning* and the use of student data. There was a common understanding across the vast majority of schools that student data should be a central aspect of school practice. In low-achieving contexts, LEPP work was focused on the development or transfer of a student tracking system, predominantly as a means to establish the use of data in internal accountability (rather than for assessment for learning). In more advanced contexts, LEPP work included:

- students understanding the levels at which they are working, with for example a head of PE developing an innovative gold/silver/bronze approach to students' understanding of curriculum levels;
- students accessing and reviewing their progress, for instance, with a school VLE personalized to users, so that students and parents could access real time information on 'my attendance' and 'my grades';
- teachers analysing student attainment data to identify learning needs and then, crucially, reviewing their own teaching strategies.

Third, *curriculum content and wider pathways*, to provide greater interest and enjoyment, increased challenge and/or re-engagement for students. Leading Edge Partnership Programme work included:

- widening student pathways and curricular options with the development of a substantial work-related learning offer and 14 to 16 qualifications provided collaboratively across the partnership in hospitality and leisure, hair and beauty, construction and engineering;

- raising the profile of a subject and building the confidence of students, for example, in languages, with the use of cross-curricular whole-school European days as well as a travelling French theatre to engage students in the practical use of language.

Fourth, *support and motivation* to provide additional care and guidance to students and to remove barriers to learning, often through (multi-agency) partnerships beyond the schools. This included:

- re-engaging students at risk of disaffection, with students making learning walks and attending a collaborative pupil conference to develop a 'Hear me out' document about what they perceived to be effective teaching, supportive environments and lessons for learning (as a resource for both CPD and initial teacher training);
- provision for gifted and talented students, with secondary staff working with primary school partners to share their subject specialisms and develop extension activities for gifted and talented students in science and mathematics.

Fifth, *school organization*, with school leaders and teachers thinking creatively about the way the school was structured and organized so that it could become more responsive to student needs and interests. This included:

- student voice and more student ownership of change, with a reorganization of the timing of the day for two lunchtimes and less queuing, an upgrade of displayed work, and a re-appraisal of a rewards system;
- transfer to secondary school, for instance with a transition teacher working for the second half of the year in primary schools undertaking withdrawal work and, then, for the first half of the following year in the secondary school, providing tailored support for students at risk, parent liaison and a friendly adult face.

While these innovations or strategies were occurring across different partnerships, there was a high degree of similarity in their aspiration to personalize learning. Moreover, there was also a relatively widely shared understanding of how Leading Edge work might contribute to developing this in practice. Drawing intuitively from the case studies, as well as conceptually from the DCSF framework of personalized learning that we were closely involved in developing, we summarize this shared approach in Figure 4.1. The diagram shows strategies building outwards around personalized learning through (1) tailoring teaching to individual need and interest; (2) supporting engagement in the classroom with curricular choice, motivation and mentoring; and (3) at a whole-school level, ensuring school organization is creatively responsive to students and underpinned by sufficient leadership and workforce capacity and competence.

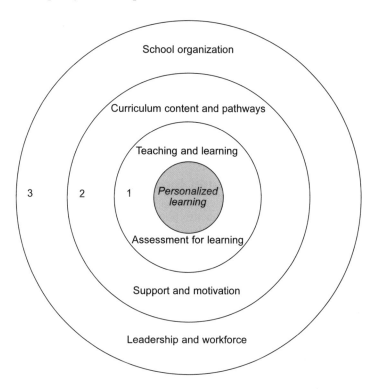

Figure 4.1 Approach to personalized learning

The diagram also makes the broader case that personalizing learning is at its most powerful when different aspects of practice fit together. Specific LEPP innovations can also be interpreted in this way. By being brought together with other school improvement strategies, for example with specialisms, curriculum reviews and other partnership work, LEPP schools can develop a coherent approach to innovation and improvement. This will be constructed differently in each context, but in our research, where there was evidence of such coherence, there was also a sense that schools were employing Leading Edge to 'work their way though problems of instructional practice at ever-increasing levels of complexity and demand' (Elmore 2004: 254). Where coherence was absent or less developed, it seemed more probable that LEPP work was a stand-alone or bolt-on innovation and hence an interesting practice that was limited to one or two departments and those directly involved.

We also note that the range of innovations detailed above did not present themselves as strikingly new (at least from a systemic perspective). There were some very impressive developments in the use of ICT, as well as in curricular pathways and the re-engaging of students in their learning. However, as a whole, the innovations to date might best be considered as incremental improvements rather than significant change in the way education is conceived and delivered. This is not necessarily a criticism, especially where partnership working was focused on taking several joint priorities to a deeper and more authentic level of inquiry. Having established working relations, the process of developing and sustaining greater depth was often an ongoing leadership and methodological challenge.

Transferring knowledge and innovating collaboratively

Two main methodological approaches were apparent in how collaborative work was being undertaken. The first concerned *the direct transfer of practice* from the lead to a partner school. This was usually as a lever for school improvement, especially in partnerships with historically low-achieving schools, those in formal improvement categories or both. There were strong parallels here to what Fielding et al. (2005) termed the 'delivery of "validated" packages of pre-formed practice seen by others to be good for the recipient'. Fielding et al. critique such knowledge transfer as having 'little validity amongst teachers'. However, in the majority of LEPP cases where this was occurring, the partner school's leadership team had actively sought out such support from their lead school. They were often trusted and seen as capable of providing effective solutions. Moreover, rather than simply being a one-off transfer of knowledge, the structure provided by Leading Edge often meant that this was an ongoing process that included a period of refinement in which transferred practice was developed into the new context. The lead schools also reported the benefits of such development work and, in several cases, reincorporated partner school ideas back into their own practices.

These were examples of success. There may have been cases where such transfer had not been effective or sustained in practice. Instances of such experience were implied to us but, more commonly, obstacles to knowledge transfer were discussed. These included:

- a partner school pulling away from collaboration when it experienced difficulties;

- a partner not wanting to receive transferred practice and/or considering (rightly or wrongly) the lead school's practice to (only) be effective when serving students from different (and usually more advantaged) backgrounds;
- the lead school not actively seeking to engage in knowledge transfer and/or the partnership's culture being at odds with such work.

The second and more typical approach to partnership working was *collaborative innovation*. This fits well with Fielding et al.'s (2005) alternative concept of 'co-construction' and the useful notion of a 'mutuality of the process' of innovation. Here, a wide range of methods was being employed across the partnerships. These included:

- *a series of informal planning meetings*, with subsequent experimentation and feedback cycles, and staff from each school discussing ideas before returning to their own classrooms to trial new approaches. The content of these new approaches was often proposed and researched by individual teachers in turn, with associated resources provided for others to trial;
- *'learning walks'*, as inspired by the Pittsburgh Institute, that included the processes of identifying a focus, undertaking a walk with observation and dialogue, giving feedback and then, crucially, undertaking a project in one's own department or school, informed by the insights gained. In several cases learning walks were being used as a means of looking inwards at departmental practices and to 'system gaze' for new ideas and inspiration and to validate one's own practice. Learning walks were also undertaken internally and externally by students as part of a student voice strategy;
- *formal research*, with one partnership in particular encouraging teachers to undertake in-school research to diploma and Master's levels under supervision from colleagues at a local university. Staff chose subjects of personal interest but also a fit within the schools' development plans and about three staff in each school per year were funded by LEPP resources. In the lead school, research opportunities had also been extended to students, with several gifted and talented students researching provision for such students, as a means to give greater rigour to student voice;
- *innovation trios*, described by a lead school as 'three members of staff who are involved with the same teaching group but in three different subjects. Together they can build a better understanding of pedagogy for those groups and support each other in their teaching'. The aspiration is for dissemination to occur through video toolkits that summarize the findings for other teachers;

- *conferences for staff* that a number of partnerships used at the end of a term or project strand to conclude and disseminate findings.

Across these methods, the identification and validation of whether new practices had been effective were predominantly based on professional judgement. This was variously described as:

- 'a gut feeling during teaching';
- 'the reaction of students as to whether they were engaged';
- 'professional dialogue at review meetings'.

Some went further to structure the use of student tracking in projects as well as more formal reporting. However, a key question many leaders were asking themselves was how to maintain authentic professional engagement, and the positive impact of informal networking, while bringing greater rigour into their LEPP approach. In particular, their concern was for evaluating the impact on student outcomes and documenting innovation so that it could be shared at a wider school level. The answer was inevitably contextual, but there was an emerging consensus across several partnerships on what greater rigour might look like. With some degree of inductive development from the actual case study practices, a model of how this might be developed is summarized in Figure 4.2.

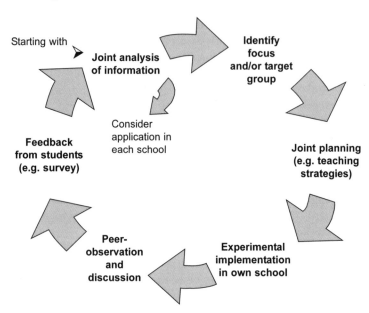

Figure 4.2 Innovating collaboratively

The process of collaborative innovation is likely to be far messier in practice than in the proposed cycle above. It is also a process governed by professional judgement and the cycle is not conceived as a strict flow but, rather, as a guide with openness to steps being rearranged or leading backwards. Each step is seen, however, to have its own value, with:

- *analysis of information*: bringing together professional judgement, contextual data, student voice, external information and research evidence to jointly interrogate current practice across the partnership;
- *identification of the focus or a target group*: with analysis leading to the collaborative development of aims and methods, be that at a whole-school level, a specific department or a classroom, but with a common theme across the schools;
- *joint planning of strategies*: with time for the key teachers and school leaders to come together to plan collaboratively the strategies or interventions;
- *experimental implementation in one's own classroom/school*: with individual project members trialling and adapting the innovations in their own contexts;
- *peer observation and feedback*: with opportunities for individuals to observe each other and discuss their experimental implementation;
- *feedback from students*: with students engaged either as respondents (through surveys or questioning) or as researchers themselves;
- (back to) *analysis of information*, with this completion of the cycle focusing on reflection and evaluation of implementation;
- (after one or more loops, potentially) the wider *applicability to each school* with either the sharing of innovation with a group of departmental or cross-curriculum colleagues or the development of a new whole-school practice.

This approach, or similar approaches in practice, is strongly aligned to the research evidence on *action research*.[1] Kemmis and McTaggart (1988), for instance, proposed a circular planner for action research which comprises the steps: Plan, Act, Observe, Reflect (and back to Plan again).[2] Hopkins (2008) proposes a set of principles to guide classroom research by teachers. These include:

- that research should not disrupt a commitment to teaching as a primary focus;
- that data collection must not be too demanding on a teacher's time;
- that the methodology employed must be reliable enough to enable the formation of hypotheses and to develop strategies for classroom practice;

- that the research focus should be one to which the teacher is committed.

These are important guidelines that would have found acceptance among a majority of Leading Edge partnerships. Several partnerships, for instance, were developing approaches that: ensured time for collaboration, appointed a LEPP coordinator in each school to support teachers, and/or developed a clear process for accessing project resources. The latter included a bidding process, funded innovation groups or, simply, devolution to one central project.

Leading innovation partnerships

These were enablers of collaboration but were insufficient in and of themselves. For it was leadership that appeared central to developing a collaborative impact on student outcomes. In particular, the commitment of senior leaders was needed to:

- sustain rigour, resources and the pro-activity of teachers and leaders with little time;
- commit both the school and partnership to a long-term engagement, despite other priorities that might come along;
- provide the *system leadership* needed to generate a partnership's purpose, direction and ethos of mutual improvement.

Where such leadership was apparent, the skills and tasks to be most clearly implicated – that we now explore in turn – were:

- building greater capacity collaboratively;
- developing new leaders and leadership models;
- facilitating lateral accountability; and
- creating a partnership vision and design for mutual improvement.

Building capacity

The language of building capacity for improvement is relatively widespread across schools (if not always well defined). The Leading Edge partnerships identified a range of capacity-building components from their collaborative practice. These included:

- developing the competence and motivation of (groups of) staff and students;

- supportive relationships, both informal and formal, nurtured by partners;
- well established systems and procedures for collaboration;
- a staff culture of sharing practice and inquiry and of talking about the quality of teaching and learning;[3]
- the alignment of professional development to support innovation;
- wider experiences of leadership for a range of staff (and students).

These had parallels to the three-part conception of capacity proposed by Hargreaves (2001) as (simply put):

- intellectual capital: the knowledge, skills and competence of staff (as well as students, parents and the community);
- social capital: with trust, relationships, networks and professional communities;
- organizational capital: the ability to mobilize resources for improvement.

Building these capacities through collective practice usually required senior leaders to commit existing resources, particularly in the initial years. Delegated funding for LEPP covered some of this but, in the majority of cases, schools also needed to deploy their own resources. This often took the form of staff time and goodwill, the use of whole-school in-service training days, the provision of specific training courses and, inevitably, staff knowledge, skills and leadership resources. These investments came with a higher than usual level of risk, given reliance on other partners. Indeed, each partnership had experienced events that depleted the emerging capacity among schools. These included:

- the unexpected shocks of key staff lost to long-term illness or to career progression elsewhere;
- the unravelling of projects following a new headteacher or leadership team arriving in one of the schools but with different priorities;
- the energy drained by a lack of full engagement by one or more partners;
- the diminishing of trust from the souring of relationships.

New models of leadership

In response, the challenge a number of leaders were facing, particularly in lead schools, was how to become more flexible, more able to engage externally and less vulnerable to staff turnover or changing priorities in partnership schools. The response, in several more advanced partnerships, had been to analyse the way in which they could bring together three relatively common concepts in educational leadership. These were:

- *system leadership* that, in these contexts, concerned leading beyond their individual schools to contribute to the wider local level through sophisticated collaboration and lateral innovation;
- *distributed leadership* to effectively orchestrate the skills of colleagues, draw them into the decision-making process and, in doing so, build their ability to take on wider leadership roles at the whole-school level (Arnold 2006);[4]
- *leadership of learning* with the focus this implies on the classroom and 'what constitutes effective learning, how the process of learning takes place, and how teaching and new technologies and tools of learning are best harnessed to support learning' (Stoll 2001: 6).

The way these concepts were being brought together can be summarized in Figure 4.3.

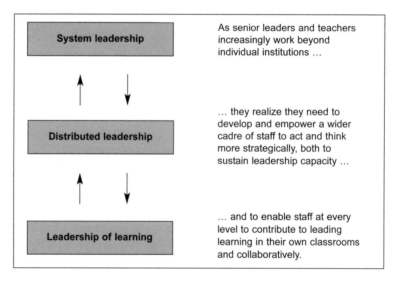

Figure 4.3 Leadership for collaborative capacity-building

There were several strong examples of this narrative in practice. In one lead school, for example, where the senior leadership team was already central to the leadership of several other local partnerships, the headteacher had developed an 'extended leadership group'. This included existing and aspirant assistant heads who met the headteacher as a reading group, with discussion designed to coach them in strategic whole-school thinking skills.

Subsequently, individuals were given responsibility for specific ('bite-size') senior leadership tasks. In another lead school, senior leaders also stressed the importance of developing middle leaders. This had occurred through external training programmes, but, more crucially, through on-the-job empowerment and ownership. This included curriculum managers writing their own sections for the school's self-evaluation form and improvement plans and meeting as the Management of Quality Teaching and Learning Group to take greater responsibility for monitoring and improving classroom practice.

Lateral accountability

While leadership development was thus a key to sustaining both internal school capacity and partnership working, collaboration had also presented the challenge of holding partners to account. This was an important part of the system leadership role, but a common concern was that doing so could damage longer-term relationships. The issues at hand were often complex and had emerged over time. These included:

- the apathy of one or more partner schools, including through absenteeism at meetings and events or a gradual unwillingness to fulfil agreed actions;
- to a lesser extent, concern expressed by partner schools about the ethos of the partnership, including the approach and focus of work, a perceived lack of support from the lead or uncertainty about how all funding was deployed.

For several partnerships, the solution lay in clearer lateral accountability. Invariably, this meant clearer expectations on issues of engagement and on developing benchmarks for progress. The strategies being developed by partnership leaders, either individually in lead schools or collectively with partner schools, included:

- more flexible involvement in specific activities, with not all schools needing to engage in every project. This appeared to work well as a response to schools who were experiencing contemporary difficulties, particularly so that they could regain fuller engagement at a later date;
- a clarification of expectations with, at the most unambiguous, a minimum number of agreed yearly activities to be undertaken by each school;
- the holding back of LEPP funding by the lead school where specific actions had not been completed by individual partner schools;
- inactive partners being left out when the partnership changed focus

or moved to a new phase (for example, following re-designation of the lead school).

These newer mechanisms were seen to be supported at a systemic level by the Leading Edge programme team at the SSAT. This included:

- at conferences, the encouragement of an equal distribution of funds and the support of school improvement for low-achieving partners;
- through the annual cycle of LEPP planning and self-evaluation, a requirement for an agreement on targets for action; and,
- through Partnership Leaders' visits, now organized for a cadre of 30 or so lead school headteachers to visit all 212 partnerships across the country with a focus on current innovative activities and the progress of partner schools. This can be seen as an emerging form of lateral accountability at the wider national level.

This was no coincidence. A clear message from the SSAT central team has been that the government expects partnerships to demonstrate measurable gains for students, especially in attainment in English and mathematics. A difficult balance for the SSAT leadership to strike is between encouraging innovation and risk-taking at the 'leading edge' and holding schools accountable for impact on student attainment – particularly given the high public profile of key performance indicators. Recently this has also come to include the importance of lead schools being re-designated as a High Performing Specialist School. Those that fall out of this category, through a set of lower exam results, will lose their Leading Edge status and funding even if their partnership is both strong and productive.

Partnership ethos and design

At the local level, perhaps the most powerful form of lateral accountability is a widely shared collaborative ethos for mutual improvement. This is the conviction that partnerships should be collegial and have an impact on the identified needs of all partners. It was thus interesting that nearly every school readily dismissed the preceding 'Beacon' model as being problematic or flawed.

This was investigated further, with all senior leaders asked to reflect on the four main types of Beacon-partner models as identified by the evaluation of the Beacon programme by the National Foundation for Educational Research (Rudd et al. 2002). These were:

- dissemination: lead school with a solution looks for partners with the original problem;

- consultancy: a customized approach to an identified problem;
- improving together: creating networks of mutual support for excellence;
- brokerage: finding solutions for requests for help.

The vast majority of leaders quickly identified, without being explicitly asked to do so, 'networks of mutual support for improvement' as a good or close description of their own partnership approach (with one also including 'consultancy'). This did not imply an abdication of leadership by the lead schools. In all cases, they set the agenda for the partnership, but usually collaboratively. They would, for instance, identify a focus and then encourage partners jointly to develop a shared approach with specific work strands. This required good relationships and trust. Most importantly, it also concerned moral purpose to share expertise and resources, particularly with partners in need.

Making this a reality was one of the clearest tasks of system leadership in innovation partnerships. Two further practical dimensions emerged. First, system leaders worked to make connections between partner schools, engage them in wider networks and use the Leading Edge partnership as a lever for wider strategic local leadership. In one partnership in Christchurch, for example, the lead school, Twynham, was at the heart of a range of local collaborations aimed at improving outcomes for students across schools in the area. The collaborations included wider learning pathways from 14 to 19, multi-agency learning support and provision for school-centred initial teacher training. Twynham's senior leadership team was a driver for many of these developments and for the involvement of partner schools in them. It also provided mentoring and support for two partner schools that had recently both come out of formal improvement categories.

Without such system leadership, the Leading Edge model can become less collegial, with partner schools rarely working directly with each other. As Figure 4.4 illustrates, in these cases collaborative work is usually channelled only through the lead school.

A second dimension to an ethos of mutual improvement was the deployment of LEPP funds. There is a concern that schools can become part of LEPP to gain wider resources without having a commitment to their appropriate use. Examples include the partner school receiving resources but taking no action, or the lead school retaining a majority of the funds with a clear rationale for doing so. Of course, where funding is not distributed equally, the lead school is quickly open to the criticism of supporting its own activities at the cost of progress in lower-achieving partners (often in more challenging circumstances). Yet such analysis would have proved unsatisfactory in all of our case studies. For, while the principle of supporting equity provides a powerful guideline, this is not solely about the distribution of funds. System

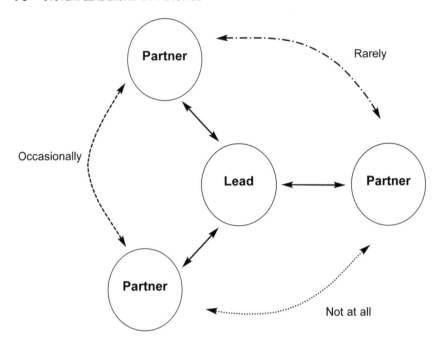

Figure 4.4 A less collegial Leading Edge partnership model

leadership seems to equate more directly to how a partnership enables the full involvement and ownership by partner schools (Reynolds 2004); how capacity for progress is built in practice; and, ultimately, whether student outcomes are improved. On these grounds, there may be cases where an unequal distribution of funds needs to be challenged. Equally, however, it may sustain the close involvement of a lead school in a partner's improvement.

Coda: system leadership across partnerships

Enhancing learning and teaching is a key priority for school leadership. Trends towards personalizing learning to individual student needs and interests, coupled with a greater responsibility for student well-being, represent real challenges for school leaders as they attempt to continue to raise school standards and offer a broad, balanced and engaging education. To meet these challenges we believe we have shown in this chapter how innovation and improvement partnerships can offer part of the solution. In particular, they can help to:

- build professional learning communities, within and across schools, that develop and widen learning and teaching strategies to respond to a range of student learning needs;

- use the full potential of school workforces to share and innovate practice, create new curricular and learning pathways and extend services before and after the school day (that we go on to explore in detail in the next chapter);
- develop new models of leadership to distribute appropriately an increasing range of responsibilities to a wider and differentiated pool of leadership expertise.

Achieving this collaborative advantage is greatly advanced by system leadership. Of course, not all innovation partnerships or, in our case here, Leading Edge partnerships will be led by system leaders. In some schools there is not the willingness to work for the success of partners. In others there is a lack of leadership capability or whole-school capacity. In these cases, collaborative progress can be made, but it may often be a harder task and/or less widespread across the partnership. Where system leadership does exist, it appears to be correlated with more advanced collaborative organization, the fuller involvement of partner schools and a greater potential for an impact on student outcomes. The thrust for such system leadership is usually provided by the lead school's leadership team. But partner schools are also involved, either in what we might call system working, as a spur to improve their own provision, or in more collaborative system leadership. Above all, collegial partnerships show clearly that system leadership is rarely delivered by one headteacher alone.

5   Leadership in the context of Every Child Matters: extended, full service and community schools

The death of a young girl as a result of appalling abuse and neglect while the family was in the radar of social services shocked a nation and provoked both recrimination in the public services and legislation intended to minimize the possibility of anything similar happening again. The outcomes were a policy focused on the needs, interest and entitlement of individual children and young people, Every Child Matters (Treasury 2003), and the related Children's Act. These measures have had radical consequences for the work, leadership and organization of schools, other public services and local authorities. In particular, it has added a new dimension to local leadership concerned with specific kinds of partnership and integrated working. This is predicated on a professional willingness and capacity to lead a wider or more complex range of provision than the discrete school unit. It can already include partnerships of groups of schools, multi-disciplinary agencies and the local authority children's services department.

In this chapter we explore such system leadership from four angles. Our analysis is based on a sample of six extended schools, covering all ages and stages of education, and three emergent local authority children and young people's trusts. First, we begin by considering the grass-roots challenges of a case study school serving a challenging local community and its efforts to support children's learning by tackling some of the social issues which were succeeding in disrupting their lives. Second, we consider how such leadership can be conceived as brokering and shaping networks of provision within and across local schools, agencies and communities so as to personalize social care and education for students and their families. Given that such welfare needs continue across the 0–19 age range, this is exemplified with reference to a diverse range of settings, including extended community provision in primary and secondary phases, extended and full-service schools and a pioneering Children and Families Trust. Third, we contrast provision for child and family with the traditional view of community education, exploring two contrasting paradigms. The ECM agenda, we argue, has shifted the focus of the school in its community from informal community links, and in some schools the provision of community education, to a clear focus on children, young people and parenting, and coherent multi-agency support. Fourth, we explore the new infrastructure in which education departments have been replaced with children and young people's services departments and trusts, with implications for system-wide and integrated service leadership.

Finally, the chapter discusses a range of characteristics and skills that effective leaders of extended schools, as system leaders, share in pursuit of the new, child-focused objectives. We argue that this will involve, increasingly, the leadership of an integrated service whose remit is wider than just education, spanning a range of professional skills. It will also become apparent that it is not axiomatic that the leadership in question necessarily stems from the largest element, the school, although in practice that generally will be the case. Above all, these leaders recognize that, for children and young people to attain their full potential, they and their families often require access to a wide range of opportunities and support to help overcome barriers to learning – especially for those living with poverty, disadvantage and disability. They also realize that putting the interests of the child first means not only providing a good school but also coordinating or integrating the range of services that relate to that child and their family.

Removing barriers to education and threats to children's well-being

Coleshill Heath Primary School, was an urban junior school for 7- to 11-year-olds when the headteacher arrived. He could hardly have faced greater challenges. The school is in one of the most socially and economically deprived areas of the country. The first governors' meeting focused on how to repair the roof and 500 broken windows. Elements of the troubled local community were described as 'angry, offensive and aggressive'. Two neighbouring blocks of flats had a notorious reputation. The school was in crisis. It lacked leadership or balanced staffing: strong male teachers had been promoted and female teachers tended to move on. The school was engulfed in issues concerning parents and children, related to crime, drugs and child protection and referrals to social services. About 90 per cent of the working population was unemployed. The school could not cope; teaching was lacklustre and relationships in the classroom were poor. The school was entrenched and besieged.

The headteacher knew that the school had to engage with the community if it was to function. Raising standards was initially way down the list of priorities. His initial range of strategies included: developing mini-rugby locally, getting fathers engaged in achieving preliminary coaching awards; using parent volunteers in school and providing them with training opportunities; raising money to help families that would otherwise resort to theft, and listening and talking to parents to learn their views of the school and the challenges they faced.

Amalgamation of the infant and junior schools offered an opportunity to provide childcare and develop the school's increasingly influential relationship with the community. A youth club was formed, involving community volunteers. Parents increasingly helped in the school. The campus became used and funded for adult training, including some degree courses. The school appointed a specialist support manager. Volunteers helped build the day nursery, which was never subsequently vandalized. A day worker linked up with families in crisis, and was influential in getting their children to school. This heavy focus on social work gradually transformed the school in its community, and made learning possible for children in appalling circumstances, so that teachers could concentrate on their teaching. System leadership in this first phase concentrated on creating an environment in which the school could get on with its core purpose of educating children. This done, the emphasis moved to learning and the school was becoming much more effective. The greatest educational challenge was getting staff of the right quality. The school invested in training, built a leadership team, and became a partner school with the local university's School of Education. This led to a stronger pool of trainee teachers from which to recruit.

The headteacher's vision was of a school that had to succeed, and would do so through meeting the problems and challenges of the community, dealing with these in a human way, involving parents to the maximum extent possible and achieving conditions in which learning could take place. By March 2005, the full-service extended school activities at Coleshill Heath included:

- *childcare*: provided year-round from 0700 to 1800;
- *health and social care*: with child/family support worker, health promotion and education (for young mums and dads), smoking cessation clinics, ante- and post-natal support, teenage advice centre and many other services;
- *lifelong learning*: organized by the local college and open all year;
- *parenting support*: on an individual and group basis;
- *study support*: including breakfast club, learning mentors, Easter and summer schools;
- *sport, arts and ICT provision*: open to all with online provision on site.

A range of other services followed. All are facilitated by the Community Co-ordinator, via the community Focus Group, made up of representatives from the local community, voluntary and statutory groups. The vision and leadership of the headteacher are highly regarded by the local authority and visiting inspectors. The staff are totally committed to developing and sustaining a strong and positive culture for academic success. The headteacher has built effective teams and leadership capacity. Like other headteachers, he has done a lot with 'bits of money', and has appointed a manager to deal with the complexity of different funding streams and lines of accountability.

Inspection of the school by Ofsted in 2008 found that pupils at the school are highly motivated by the additional services provided. They enjoy attending school and feel their views are valued. The raising of self-esteem, attainment and rate of progress is fully supported by the multi-professional approach established. Educational standards have improved steadily each year. Pupils have very positive attitudes to their work, respond enthusiastically to challenge and competition, behave exceptionally well in school and are respectful to adults.

On the basis of this historical transformation, it was natural that the school became a leading light in what is now the local authority's 'hub and spoke' model of a cluster of five schools (Dunkley et al. 2005). Coleshill Heath is the hub, providing not only an extended day but also a full range of support services covering social care, health, community policing, adult learning and other services. It is the centre of a structured network with other schools, through which expertise and a range of services for children and families are shared. The headteacher is now engaged in area-wide system leadership for 80 per cent of his time while his deputy is acting headteacher of the school.

Extended schools, Full Service schools and networks or clusters

System leaders have influence beyond their immediate bailiwick. Coleshill Heath was a pathfinder for the government's extended schools project, in which schools provide not only education but day care beyond school hours. Extended schools originate from ideas set out in the Schools Plus Report (DfEE 1999).The policy of extended schools is intended by the government to help achieve its objective of lifting children out of poverty and improving outcomes for them and their families. In the belief that educational attainment is a powerful route out of poverty and disadvantage, a priority for schools is to reach the most disadvantaged families within a universal framework of providing mainstream services for all families. By 2010, all primary schools are expected to become extended schools, providing access to childcare and a varied menu of activities from 0800 to 1800, five days a week, for 48 weeks a year. Secondary schools must provide access to a varied menu of activities which also offers young people a safe place to be from 0800 to 1800 during term-time and more flexibly in the holidays (DCSF 2007b).

The policy of the extended school is at the heart of the Every Child

Matters agenda which charges all schools to raise standards and ensure that children:

- are healthy;
- stay safe;
- enjoy and achieve;
- make a positive contribution;
- achieve economic well-being.

The NCSL's extended schools network provides a vehicle for professional development, sharing knowledge, and disseminating good practice in the development of extended and full-service schools.[1] The role of the individual school leader should not be overlooked amid the stream of system-level developments. Not only have school leaders been pivotal in giving life to these initiatives, but they have often seen the need and led the way in advance of policies and funding.

As we have seen, many schools like Coleshill Heath have been providing extended services for some time and the coordinated provision of services within a cluster of schools is increasingly common. Some schools have the full range of coordinated or integrated provision based on site. One in east London has over 30 on-site pupil-support staff or teams, ranging from a team dealing with complex needs to police, social workers to counsellors, health workers to youth provision.

Such schools have become known as full-service schools. The government has funded three waves of full-service extended school (FSES) projects starting in 2003 and eventually including 148 schools. The funding aims to promote further development of support services for young people and their parents. Developments have been more recent and pronounced in primary schools, and in the foundation stage where Sure Start[2] moves towards full-service provision, building on the nursery education that is a common feature of schools in this sector. A major evaluation of this initiative (Cummings et al. 2007) found that many schools and their partner agencies saw it as an opportunity to bring together a wide range of efforts to meet the challenge facing themselves, their pupils and the communities they served. Schools showed considerable effort and ingenuity in developing their provision. However, FSES pose significant challenges for schools in terms of managing this provision alongside all the other demands on leadership teams: establishing productive partnerships with other agencies and providers, and finding ways of making provision sustainable.

We have found that great enthusiasm, dedication to making multi-agency partnerships work and optimism are only partially successful in making cohesive provision. Major barriers are not a lack of cooperation but the practicalities of combining the efforts of different professional groups working under great disparities of pay and conditions. The FSES evaluation found that leadership and management were most effective where schools had a senior member of staff who acted as FSES coordinator or in other ways integrated FSES responsibility within their leadership structure. Schools tended to be the dominant partners, other member agencies being consulted rather than being given a full say in decision-making although there are notable exceptions to this, where the leadership recognizes all the partners as essential parts of the system.

The impact of extended and full-service schools on standards is not established with any certainty. Cummins et al. (2007: 3) find that 'an FSES approach is likely to be associated with improved school performance, better relations with local communities and an enhanced standing of the school in its area, though it is also likely that other factors will contribute to these outcomes'. Sammons et al. (2003) found no significant differences in outcomes when comparing Scottish New Community Schools with other schools. The government claims that results improved at twice the national average in the first wave of full-service extended schools. It is possible that the effect owes something to these pilot schools being better led and managed than the average. In some of our case studies, particularly in primary schools such as Coleshill Heath, becoming an extended school has categorically improved the conditions for learning and can be associated with improved achievement.

The changing role of the school in its community

The roots of education-led community leadership were strongly established in many schools before being overlaid by ECM. Community colleges[3] and schools have their origins in the work of Henry Morris, Education Secretary to Cambridge from 1922 to 1954, whose vision (Morris 1924) allowed him to expand the idea of rural secondary schools into the concept of Community Colleges. The buildings would house the school during the day and then provide educational, cultural and leisure opportunities for adults during the evening: the foundations of lifelong learning. Cambridgeshire community colleges include Sawston and Impington Village Colleges, which continue in the Morris tradition. Cambridgeshire community colleges have their imitators in many parts of England. Community high schools in Northumberland, for example, combine school, adult and youth provision within their purview and others, for example Challney Boys School and Community College in Luton, have moved to an extended day timetable in which students and parents can learn together in the evening.

A further impetus for community education has been provided by urban regeneration schemes. Recent government initiatives have ensured that provision for young children is catching up fast with the community ideal for secondary schools. Sure Start and the experiment in Early Excellence Centres have paved the way for Children's Centres. Foremost among these policies is Every Child Matters and the ten-year strategy from HM Treasury of support for children and families. The emergent Children and Young People's Trusts represent, in our case studies, a vision of integrated provision at system level.

A classification of the school–community dynamic

Rather than focusing on origins and evolution, the case study examples of community or extended schools or networks suggest a typology which captures the dimensions of these systems. Two axes can be used to reflect aspects of the school's mission that look, first, at the internal–external locus of learning and, second, at the human focus, ranging from the needs of individual children and young people to those of the community. This is expressed in Figure 5.1. At the centre lies the fundamental core business of the school, traditionally defined by curriculum, teaching, learning and assessment.

The original community schools, such as the 'village colleges' of Cambridgeshire referred to earlier, primarily reflected a vision of the school as a resource for learning in the community. Such schools would be represented strongly in quadrant 'C' in Figure 5.1. The community school in this sense is well established. Its core work is the education of its enrolled learners, but it also provides adult education and services for youth. There is a measure of integration, not found with the separately led and managed 'adult institutes' of schools whose premises are used for evening classes. There is little crossover in such schools, whereas in community schools, courses can be accessed by adults as well as young people. Many community secondary schools, such as those in Northumberland, include a further deputy headteacher (community) in the senior leadership team. Their status in the team can vary, but they can have a prominent and influential role in an outward-looking school.

The thrust of full-service extended schools is strongly represented by quadrant 'A' which develops support for child and family learning on site or within a network or partnership. Many Early Excellence Centres did this successfully for young children and their families. These are well documented (Andreae and Matthews 2006) and led to the establishment of children's centres and related providers. Some centres encompass not only childcare, nursery education – and, in some cases, primary schooling – and adult learning, but also family support, social service and health provision. Schools having a high component of 'A' reflect a dedication to the Every Child Matters agenda. Many of the services associated with extended and full-service schools fall into quadrant A.

Schools that are reflected prominently in 'B' are typified by rich extra-

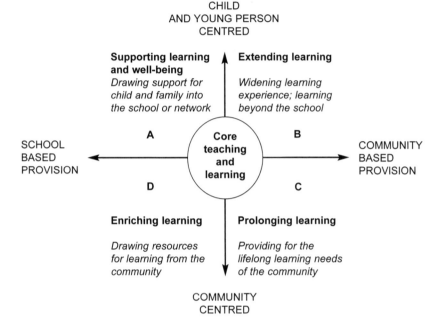

Figure 5.1 A simple classification of the school-child-community relationship
Source: Matthews 2006a: 6.

curricular and outreach activities, including outdoor and environmental education, Duke of Edinburgh's Award, international links and exchanges and other features that use the locality, region, country or globe to extend educational experience and relevance.

Most schools have an element of 'D' by drawing community resources into the school to enrich learning. An example drawn from a northern primary school typifies the many schools that exhibit this dimension strongly, for example in relation to the promotion of health, safety and well-being. Its inspection found that theatre groups are well used by the school to support drugs education. The school nurse effectively raises awareness of health issues and frequently gives talks and advice to pupils. She also supports sex education by giving talks for Year 6 pupils. The community police officer attends the school regularly and talks to pupils about 'stranger danger', road safety, and citizenship. A recent talk from a building contractor concerned safety on building sites. The school has implemented a very good quality health and safety policy. Partnerships with parents and the community are very good and make a significant and positive impact on pupils' attainment. The school positively encourages and welcomes parents to become involved in school life. The home-school liaison officer makes an invaluable contribution to developing links with parents and the community. The Parents' Centre provides many opportunities for parents to become involved in school life. The Parents' Association provides valuable support for the school through fundraising. A few parents help in school regularly, working effectively with staff. They assist in classrooms, listen to pupils read, help with extra-curricular activities such as netball and rounders, and accompany school trips.

All schools are likely to reflect all quadrants or characteristics to a greater or lesser extent. The extended school, for example, will be strong on *supporting learning,* whatever else it does. The balance between components A, B, C and D will shift, depending on the type and context of the school. Self-evaluation against this classification provides a means by which schools can consider whether they have an underdeveloped area in relation to the children, families and communities they serve. Figure 5.2 shows schematic profiles of four providers in terms of their relative emphases reflected by the four quadrants in Figure 5.1.

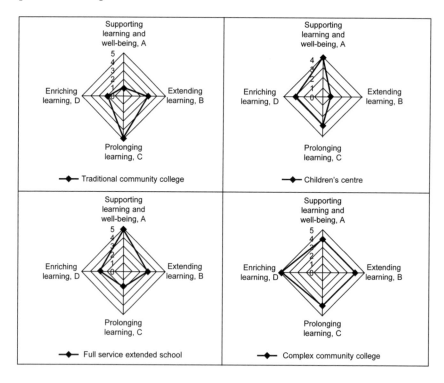

Figure 5.2   Profiles of four providers in terms of the school-child-community relationship

Schools like the Coleshill Heath example are very effectively resolving any tension between A and C by providing for adult learning which engages parents in the school and supports families and the community. This can only come about through a system-leading role which has the vision, courage and drive to strengthen the school through helping to develop the community. The models illustrated in Figures 5.1 and 5.2, derived from case study evidence, bring the aspects represented by A, B, C and D together through a system leadership approach needed by broad or multi-faceted providers such as extended or full-service community schools or children's centres.

Characteristics of a community-focused school

Most of the schools in the sample can be described as community-focused schools in that they represent the belief that pupils will be even more successful if their needs are addressed holistically, in particular including their family circumstances. Work in Kingston-upon-Hull has offered a useful illustration of some of the characteristics likely to be present in a community orientated school and requiring a measure of system leadership:

    i.   'Adopts a holistic approach to the needs of its pupils, sensitive to all the conditions that can affect a child's development and ability to learn.

    ii.   Views working with the community as an important element in raising the standard of pupils' achievement.

    iii.   Has a strong positive engagement with parents, carers and families to promote their role as the first and co-educators of their children.

    iv.   Responds to community need and contributes to shaping and developing the local culture, leading and/or supporting as required. Contributes to creating communities of lifelong learners.

    v.   Is a centre which either provides services directly (through co-location) or supports other services important to children and their families.

    vi.   Is recognised as a centre of learning for learners of all ages where the school's resources are at the disposal of the local community.

    vii.   Works collaboratively with other schools and with a range of complementary services.

    viii. Has a curriculum that is broad and balanced but also relevant to the needs of pupils and respectful of pupils' backgrounds and experience.'

(Kingston-upon-Hull Children's Services internal working paper, 2006)

Reform of local authority infrastructure

The drive to define and deliver the outcomes for children has resulted in radical policy developments: first to abolish local authority education and social services departments and replace them with children's services departments, responsible for the range of provision that will contribute to the five ECM outcomes for children and support for parents and families. Second, in 2007, policy matters concerned with early years care and learning, education in schools and provision for family learning were corralled into the new 'Department for Children, Schools and Families' (DCSF).

At local authority level, our study of Brighton and Hove Council shows how the Council has sought to make every child matter across the borough through the creation, in 2006, of the Brighton and Hove Children and Young People's Trust (CYPT). The Council was one of the first local authorities to respond to the challenge of Every Child Matters and was a pathfinder for Children's Trusts. In April 2002, provision for education and children's social care was merged into the cross-service Children, Families and Schools Directorate to promote the Children Act's five key outcomes for children and young people. The Ofsted/Audit Commission inspection (Ofsted 2004: 1) described the Directorate's overall effectiveness as good. 'A clear vision, explicit priorities, strong strategic capability and successful work with a number of other agencies have enabled the authority to position itself in the *forefront of national developments*...The directorate is well placed to undertake its planned transition towards a Children's Trust' (our emphasis). The Council created the Children and Young People's Trust, guided by the skilful leadership of the Directorate of Children, Families and Schools. The Director (Hawker 2006: 21) envisaged the Trust as:

> a single organisational entity bringing together the management or education, social care, youth work (including Connexions) and children's community healthcare. It will have commissioning and partnership arrangements with a range of other bodies in the statutory, voluntary and private sectors, including schools, general practitioners (GPs) and childcare providers.

The Trust brings together education, health and social care for all 0–19-year-olds. The main organizations which form the CYPT are the City Council, the local National Health Service (NHS) Primary Care and Hospital Trusts, the Police Authority and the Connexions[4] service. Details are set out in a comprehensive business plan for 2006–2009 (Brighton and Hove Council 2006). The Trust is based on the rationale that partnership working will not suffice for the significant improvement of outcomes for children and that nothing less than *structural integration* will do. This borough-wide initiative provides a promising model for replication elsewhere. The transformation from partnership to integrated arrangements is complex and demanding, and involves securing the current delivery of services while planning and implementing change if the Trust is to be fully operational from 2009.

System leadership is, clearly, crucial to the successful development of such an ambitious system. The Council's Annual Performance Assessment (APA) in 2005 found that the authority's children and families directorate demonstrates strong leadership, both operationally and politically. The authority has a well-managed strategy to complete the transition to a Children's Trust and is actively engaged with parents and young people to inform the development of its services.

We found the style of leadership to be demanding and ambitious, seeking to drive the pace of change while delegating responsibility and giving autonomy. Good communication was seen as particularly important from the point at which education and social service areas were merged. The service providers are all represented at 14 strategic partnership groups, which meet regularly to review progress, discuss and resolve issues, and reach decisions.

Challenges, opportunities and threats

Many challenges needed to be faced with any form of service integration, let alone one as far-reaching as a Trust. They started with getting all parties to subscribe to the common objective and the vision of how support for children and families might look. As the Director expressed it (interview, Summer 2006), 'putting children first requires a city-wide change of mindset'. The challenge is to show the many and varied service providers how seemingly disparate projects link to an overall plan, without causing anxiety over the number, direction and sustainability of initiatives which are promoting inclusion. In reality, these were well mapped and coherent. Careful monitoring realigned less successful aspects of provision. Keys to success appear to include: careful and participative planning; good communication to show how the parts contribute to the whole; resources matched to need; and assiduous monitoring of impact and dissemination of effective practice. The APA in 2007 recognized within the CYPT and with external partners a strong culture of multi-disciplinary teamwork at strategic and operational levels and a strong ambition to utilize these partnerships to develop its range of preventative services. The Council has made good progress in working with vulnerable groups and some that are hard to reach. Its work is well focused on improving the achievement of less advantaged children and young people, such as through the successful development of children's centres, effective support for schools causing concern and good progress made by groups such as looked after children and young people (Ofsted 2007: 9). There is no questioning the ambition and moral purpose of the Trust. Its mission is that Brighton and Hove should be the best place in the country for children and young people to grow up. As the Director said, 'we want to ensure all our children get the best possible start in life, so that everyone has the opportunity to fulfil their potential, whatever that might be'.

The outgoing Director (interview, Summer 2006) expressed the welter of objectives – or aspirations – in the Children and Young People's Plan more succinctly by giving a flavour of some of the differences that the strategic change is intended to make to children's lives:

> They will arrive at school ready to learn;
> - all will be in really good schools
> - all have access to good quality learning
> - fewer families live in inappropriate housing
> - no one can say their needs are ignored
> - children and young people feel safe and valued in the community
> - school results are above the national average
> - minimal school leavers are not in education, employment or training.

In terms of impact, early success is claimed for the extended schools strategy in which 13 schools are supported by strategy funding. Partnerships involving health and sports, and healthy eating and anti-bullying campaigns are all proving fruitful. The impact on academic outcomes is not yet evident, but children and young people express satisfaction with the way they have been consulted and feel their views are listened to. Some of the ingredients of success, which reflect the boldness which typifies much effective system leadership, are:

- listening to the voices of children, young people and families;
- putting children and families first in all their intentions;
- consulting widely and involving all partners fully;
- planning simply but strategically;
- appointing people who share or subscribe to the vision;
- building teams, training them and trusting them;
- communicating and sharing the vision and core principles and beliefs;
- not accepting that anything is impossible.

Similar models are being pursued by other CYP departments and trusts across the country. In Suffolk, for example, there is a strong emphasis on the training and development of those who provide the many different services for children and young people as a single cadre: the integrated service workforce. Some of the principles underpinning the approach are to create a culture of integrated provision; to promote parity of esteem between different types of worker; to develop an integrated qualifications framework; and to ensure that wherever practicable, training is multi-agency and multi-professional in application. The biggest threat to the effective working of trusts is potentially any lack of capacity or commitment among partners to embody the culture of integrated working envisaged by the creation of trusts.

Extended school system leaders at work

The first and most striking feature of most of the system leaders we have studied in the context of extended schools which are also 'area hubs' is that they lead by example. They are transformational, and champion child-, family- and community-focused schools, commonly having pioneered work in their own school as a necessity for the school's survival as a viable provider of education. In smaller schools, particularly, such headteachers can be short of allies when taking over the leadership of a school in challenging circumstances. Forming the 'guiding coalition' envisaged at an early stage of Kotter's change model (Coleman 2006), for example, is often preceded by a great deal of work in listening, communicating, creating and sharing a vision.

Several of the leaders considered here started from a position of relative isolation. They are invariably working in schools and communities that pose a great deal of challenge. Their courage, conviction and resilience were tested to the limit in developing a shared sense of purpose and building the teams, networks and partnerships that began to address some of the difficulties that children and families face. Leaders in the case study schools have all made a huge professional and emotional investment in the school, working passionately, persuasively and relentlessly to develop an ethos that puts the child or young person at the centre of the school's thinking. They may be averse to heroic, demonstrative or messianic leadership, but heroes they are, and a touch of charisma can help. They attract and retain staff that share their commitment and values and, in some cases, they quickly lose those that do not. In the section that follows, we discuss characteristics exhibited by the leaders in the case studies.

Vision and purpose

The first impression is of how rapidly school leaders are responding to the ECM agenda and the subsequent extended schools initiative. For some leaders, ECM came as an articulation of what they had long believed about the development and well-being of the whole child and the need to provide systemic coordinated support of different agencies rather than disjointed intervention.

The extended schools initiative came at the right time for some leaders by providing the financial boost to services they were already developing or wished to develop. It was typical of the leaders encountered that they did not rest on their laurels but knew what needed to be done next. Inevitably, their plans focused on children's needs and families that needed support. The most successful extended schools were more focused on these ECM priorities than on the wider range of provision for lifelong learning that could be supplied to the community, which they regarded as important but less central to the other services.

Entrepreneurship and strategic development

The successful leaders are those that see the need for provision that will benefit their children and young people, families and communities and strive to meet that need. The development of a Trust at Brighton and Hove is an example of visionary professional leadership working alongside strong political leadership to bring major system-wide change over a period of six or more years. No less powerful are the examples of leaders in most of the case study schools who, for much of the extended periods over which they have worked to support and better the lives of the children and families served by their schools, were quietly heroic. These leaders seized opportunities when they came and forged them when they did not, gradually building links with other services and themselves being pillars of strength and resilience in turbulent, disadvantaged and disturbed communities.

All the extended school leaders are highly entrepreneurial. They have the vision of what needs to be done but travel a difficult road to get there. Their approaches are typified by:

- networking: with other services, public and corporate bodies, the private sector, the local authority and other schools in order to register their needs and explore the opportunity for partnerships;
- bidding: for whatever funds or initiatives become available that can be harnessed to their need;
- risk-taking: by doing things that might court bureaucratic obstruction, delegating responsibility and accepting the fact that things will sometimes go wrong, and finding unorthodox solutions;
- appointing the right people: who share the ethos of the institution, offer something extra, and are committed to young people;
- securing the wholehearted backing of their governors;
- communicating effectively with children, young people, families and

the community: finding out what they want, where the pressures are in their lives, giving them a voice;
- a commitment to inclusion; where every child, parent and family really does matter.

Resource management

Strategic approaches are most feasible where leaders can control the factors that affect their destinies. In reality, this is seldom possible. The schools are reliant on multiple, changing and often short-term funding streams. Considerable time and energy are invested in bidding for various sources of finance and support. Leaders take full advantage of these while they last but inevitably have to cut back when they finish. Leaders exercised considerable energy and ingenuity in trying to make developments self-supporting or getting them adopted by partner bodies. Dunford (2006) has raised the issue of the impact of widening expectations for school services on school budgets.

There are many other challenges to the system leaders of extended, full-service schools. They make appointments to the school of workers having a range of skills, often unconnected with education. Inevitably, there are differences in pay and conditions of service relating to these different occupational areas, some of which may make sense in the provision of discrete services but can be invidious in the context of an integrated service school. Negotiation and resolution of such matters are time-consuming but important, and they are an extra drain on leaders who do not always have the skilled managerial or personnel support to hand.

Time in post

Most of the leaders encountered had long engagement with their communities. This was clearly an advantage, for they had had the time to develop the ethos of the organization, inculcating a unified approach among all workers on the school site. Some, approaching retirement age, showed no sign of diminished commitment to the mission. Some had reservations about being seconded part-time to their local authority to help extend other schools.

One of the hallmarks of the effectiveness of successful community leaders is that they build up extensive networks and strong partnerships. The communities that see what the headteacher is trying to do for them, and the lengths to which they will go to help them or their children, are likely to be both appreciative and highly supportive. Several of the headteachers visited were educating the children of parents they had taught.

The effective and valued community leader develops a commitment to the community that is reciprocated. This is a long-term and, for most in our sample, a compelling mission. As one said, 'I have worked all my lifetime in a triangle of schools within a mile and a half of each other'. This is not to say he was parochial, since engagement in national developments and networks, largely through the National College for School Leadership had broadened his vision, experience and contacts.

Team building and succession planning

Most of the headteachers in the sample had given considerable support to the professional development of their leadership teams. Typically, the deputies and assistant headteachers in secondary schools had incorporated one or more community dimensions within their leadership roles. All or most had gained the National Professional Qualification for Headship (NPQH) and had access to other high level development, such as a school-based MBA.

Capacity-building was most successful where the headteacher prepared staff or identified capability and delegated responsibility. This was apparent in one inner-city school, for example, where the community strategy was largely delegated to two highly capable assistant headteachers responsible for 'community' and 'inclusion'. They worked in close partnership, for much of the extended school provision served to support young people who faced severe domestic, social, economic or emotional barriers to learning.

Delegation went further in another urban school where a middle leader was taking forward the extended school agenda, reporting to a deputy headteacher who had overall responsibility for community education. This reflected the confidence of the headteacher in a colleague who had the commitment and skills to take on the challenge of building community partnerships and was doing so successfully.

In most of the areas visited, the skills and qualities of the community leaders have been recognized in their own local authorities, where some have been released, full- or part-time, to work to disseminate their experience across the authority. In one case, there is reportedly no authority funding and little apparent interest in the developments taking place on a shoestring in the community, in partnership with the school.

Sustainability of extended and community schools

The full-service extended school can survive only if funding for it is part of mainstream funding: in other words, the total funds required for integrated full-service provision need to be delegated to the multi-agency cost centre that is the school. Brighton and Hove Council is pioneering such an approach through the Trust development, where the biggest challenge lies in recon-ciling funding for primary health care with local authority services. The integrated provision at one case study school would be – with the addition of health – amenable to such funding, in contrast to the present situation, where the number, variable conditions and duration of funding streams are a major preoccupation of the leadership. Coordinated area provision, with advantage, could have unified funding for the full range of services in that area. The other approach taken by some extended schools is to encourage the partner provider to fund the ongoing school-based provision, its value having been demonstrated.

Community school leadership is not, it appears, a field for the leader passing through. It takes time to build links and relationships, and success appears to require durable commitment. Community schools can and do cope with change at the top. This is secured, even more than in less complex schools, by a strong leadership team and structure.

Tension between standards and ECM and how this is being reconciled in practice

In all the cases examined, there was ready acceptance of the importance of the five outcomes for children and young people and recognition that they were mutually interdependent. The ECM agenda has been absorbed by the institutions visited for the purpose of this evaluation and is the driver for the reorganization of local authorities.

The prevailing view of schools in the sample was that ECM and extended schools help promote higher standards by providing the awareness and support that contribute to reducing barriers to learning. Most schools argue for and can demonstrate a rising trend in standards and/or contextual value-added scores, as shown in the case studies.

There can be a risk that enthusiasm for building community provision can reduce the focus on raising standards. In this sense, one characteristic community school, represented by quadrant C in Figure 5.1, was distracted from raising the quality of the classroom experience which is central to much A-type provision. This secondary school faces an ongoing challenge in respect of raising standards, despite exceptional community provision. The head-teacher appeared too involved with the school's community provision to provide a strong lead in raising core standards.

Coda: the challenge for system leadership

Community leadership in the era of ECM has special complexities and makes exceptional demands. It can be envisaged that every school leader could become a leader of an extended school as their schools increasingly provide, on site or in a neighbourhood partnership, the full-service strands of extended provision. The assumption is that rounded, multi-agency or integrated support for the child, young person and family will help them to achieve to their potential. Our studies tend to support this assumption. To become effective system leaders in the terms of our definition, leaders of schools with a child, family and a community focus must be able not only to be leaders of providers but also leaders alongside others within provider partnerships. This is a case more of shared than of distributed leadership, although within the partnership there may well be a place for the lead practitioner. In terms of extended and full-service schools, the NCSL's strong network of such providers disseminates best practice and provides opportunities to access it. Key skills for the leaders of these providers include:

- an understanding of the culture and work practices of other professionals;
- a close understanding of the needs of children and families – taking account of their views – and the initiatives which will prove most helpful;
- networking, consultancy and brokering skills; and real ambition for the community which can be realized through high expectations, high standards and high quality, well directed provision.

Cross-agency working is a reality in many areas. There are opportunities for the further evolution of national programmes for multi-disciplinary development in relation to ECM and community-focused schools. The challenge for system leaders at local, area or authority level is to move from services working in partnership to full integration. It is only when there is an integrated workforce for children and young people that the cracks between agencies into which a vulnerable child can slip disappear. An integrated workforce needs a new form of system leadership. Rather than leadership *of* a partnership, the requirement is for leadership from *within* a partnership or, rather, from within integrated service provision. In all the cases examined, however, the system has moved a significant distance from its origins, driven by the current leader(s). They either embraced the vision they inherited when taking over the leadership of the institution, or – where vision was lacking – saw what had to be done, and set about doing it, often against the prevailing climate.

6   Executive leadership and federations

State schools have traditionally supported others facing difficulties through ad hoc support, headteacher secondments and local authority networks. The willingness of school leaders to help neighbouring schools was severely tested by the introduction in the late 1980s of quasi-market forces, high stakes accountability and subsequent competition in education. When a school showed signs of decline and its students started to face the consequences, it became less certain that other local public sector schools would play a role in its recovery. In this context, executive headteachers and their wider leadership teams represent a rediscovery of the traditional moral purpose that is a powerful motivational force within the teaching profession. By formalizing their support for a school facing significant difficulties, executive heads are system leaders who work for the success and welfare of students in other schools as well as in their own.

Executive headship refers to headteachers in England who lead two or more schools that have entered into a federation. A common federative model involves a lead school working to support and improve a partner school (or schools). To date, there is only a small and emerging research literature and thus no well developed analysis of how these roles are being organized. In seeking to contribute to this literature, this chapter elaborates the concepts of 'support federations' and system leadership in three main ways. First, with reference to a case study, it explores the historical and policy contexts out of which these roles have developed. Second, it analyses not only how such roles are being undertaken but also what forms of expertise and capacity are mobilized in the pursuit of another school's improvement. Third, it considers whether these leadership roles might provide alternative solutions to problems that have traditionally become the responsibility and preserve of the central apparatus of the state.

Chalvedon and Barstable as an example of a 'hard' support federation

Twenty years ago, when Alan Roach arrived as headteacher in 1988, Chalvedon school was the poor relation of Barstable school. It had been for some time. The schools were close neighbours. Both served the same housing estate community. Both had a high proportion of students from disadvantaged backgrounds. But, in that year, only 4 per cent of Chalvedon's students achieved the benchmark of five A* to C grades in the new GCSE qualification. At Barstable, about 35 per cent of students reached it. Through Alan's leadership, the hard work of staff and the increasing commitment of students, Chalvedon began a slow but steady improvement. Six years later, and for the first time, a quarter of students achieved the GCSE benchmark. It was an important result that was rightly celebrated at Chalvedon. But the popping of corks was not heard at Barstable. Only about 20 per cent of its students had achieved the benchmark that year and so, in 1994, another first was recorded. Barstable's results had fallen below Chalvedon's for the first time in as long as many local people could remember.

Barstable had lost its way a little. The headteacher who had led the school at its peak had long retired. The curriculum offer, staffing levels and resource expectations had started to become unsustainable. Standards of achievement in external examinations had dipped. Local perceptions of the school were starting to deflate. It was a very unfortunate time for these first signs of decline to appear. The significant changes introduced in the 1988 Education Act were starting to bite. The Act's language of local educational markets and consumer choice had become a reality. Clear external standards, inspections by Ofsted and examination league tables were in force. Parents, especially those from middle class backgrounds, had started to vote with their children's feet. Competition among schools for student-linked funding was in the ascendancy. The local authority's powers and capacity to provide leadership across a locality had been reduced (for all but the weakest schools, where intervention was expected and school closure a real possibility). A number of schools had also taken up the new option to be further released from local authority control by seeking Grant Maintained Status. Chalvedon had been among the first.

Fast forward a decade to 2005. A locally perceptible cycle of school decline and renewal had come half circle. Barstable had been in and out of special measures and serious weaknesses.[1] It had just achieved its lowest ever GCSE results of 10 per cent. Student behaviour was very poor. There were 17 reported cases of physical abuse of students by staff. The management of certain key areas had been judged by Ofsted to be insufficiently effective. With a shrinking student roll, Barstable was hitting rock bottom and was a candidate for closure. Chalvedon, by contrast, had just achieved its highest ever results with over half its students reaching the GCSE benchmark. Its yearly intake had grown from 260 to 330 students. The school had completed a root and branch transformation. It had developed five complementary internal systems to monitor and support student attainment, progression, attendance, behaviour and welfare across the curriculum. It had won a local regeneration bid, ahead of the local authority, for over £500,000 which it had used to lead the provision of joined-up multi-agency extended children's services across a network of 19 schools. It had also started to support the improvement of schools in other regions with similar contextual character-istics through a network facilitated by the SSAT. This had been challenging and not always successful, but Chalvedon's staff had reported gaining excellent professional development and the skills to help others. Chalvedon was on the up.

Then perhaps the most significant event in this near two-decade-long history occurred. One day in early October 2005, Alan's phone rang. The local authority wanted to know what Chalvedon could do to help Barstable. What happened next, and the more general implications it holds for large-scale system-wide renewal, is the focus of this chapter.

System renewal in England

As we saw in Chapter 1, the New Labour government and its 'Third Way' philosophy combined the forces of market competition and external stan-dards on the one hand with collaboration and the sharing of best practice on the other. The government claimed system-wide success, for instance, 'in narrowing the gap between high performing and worse performing schools ... mostly because of our zero-tolerance to failure' (Jim Knight, Minister of State for School Standards, 2007). Yet, while a range of schools in challenging circumstances has improved faster than the national average, and this should be celebrated, socio-economic disadvantage, as we saw in Chapter 3, remains a key determinant of educational achievement. Moreover, while there are now just over 250 schools in special measures, half the number of 1997, there has been a relatively continuing supply of schools over the decade entering and re-entering this formal improvement category.

Of course, sustaining improvement, achieving reliability and renewing schools before their performance peaks is difficult. There is a range of usual suspects. Lack of know-how. Change fatigue. Complacency. Unforeseen shocks. A number of key leadership retirements. No succession plans. The first few turns of a downward spiral can begin. In most cases the commitment and experience of staff and the social capital of the community can arrest or conceal decline (Elmore 2004). However, there is also a set of structural forces that may act against such agency: the impacts of market-driven competition on fragile institutions (Lamb 2007); falling rolls due to demographic changes (Taylor et al. 2000); the more general difficulty of sustaining high standards in contexts of social deprivation (Thrupp 1999; Lupton 2005).

Where such factors lead to a fall in results below national floor targets, a sequential response is laid out by the national accountability system in England. For some schools this external intervention is the wake-up call they need (NAO 2006). For others, it can lead to more superficial change or, worse, a longer-term slide into 'sink school' status (Taylor et al. 2000). In such circumstances, a key question is whether there are alternative responses to low attainment that are capable of improving teaching quality for students through more effective methodologies. In other words, what are the alternatives to intervention by central government for achieving sustainable and higher valued-added performance? In addition, in contexts where the historical fortunes of several local schools may have been inversely related, can renewal become more mutually beneficial to more than one school?

A potential answer may lie in a set of professional practices emerging in England and elsewhere.[2] In particular, this is the practice of system leadership within federations. Take, for instance, the school in special measures. Ofsted (2006a) judges that poor leadership and poor teaching are the two main reasons behind such a school's inadequacy. Strong leadership is thus vital to turn the school around and yet it is often such schools that are the least able to attract suitable leaders. Informal collaboration may provide some assistance. Yet for access to well developed school improvement intelligence and best practice in leadership, as well as to assistance in refining these practices in its own context, the school may be better served by sustained engagement with an experienced leader and the wider capabilities and capacities of the leader's school.

Chalvedon and Barstable – part two

Following the local authority's request to help Barstable, Alan, his senior leadership team and governing body agreed. But, having experienced resistant governors, insufficiently responsive senior management teams or both at the other schools they had tried to help, Chalvedon's leadership was clear on the model for support. It had to be a 'hard' federation (see the next section), in which the schools would share one governing body and clear lines of decision-making and accountability. The local authority agreed and, in late November 2005, the Chalvedon and Barstable Federation was established. At first the two headteachers continued in post with Barstable's head attempting to lead the replication of Chalvedon's systems in his own school. By Christmas, however, little progress had been made and so Alan suggested he would take on an executive headteacher post with responsibility for both schools. Barstable's head agreed with a big sigh (remembered as relief). He knew his attempts at change had been thwarted by a significant minority of resistant staff. Alan and his senior leadership colleagues were going to be more direct. In January 2006, now halfway through the academic year, a new timetable and curriculum were introduced to replace one that had not reflected actual teaching practice. The school day between the two institutions was already staggered by 15 minutes. Alan dashed back and forth. Key Chalvedon staff led the detailed replication and refinement of their own systems and practices at

Barstable. Day-to-day senior leadership at Barstable was undertaken by one of Chalvedon's deputies. Some Barstable staff gained new teaching experiences at Chalvedon. Another 22 resigned from the federation altogether during the next two terms and, in doing so, eradicated Barstable's significant over-staffing and budget deficit. Power struggles, large and small, candid and covert, continued. But change developed momentum and students respond-ed. By May, Ofsted deemed Barstable to be providing a satisfactory standard of education for the first time since placing the school in special measures five years earlier. By the summer, 28 per cent of students had achieved the GCSE benchmark, up from 12 per cent the previous year.

This is an example of how system leadership by an experienced school leader and their school might provide alternative solutions to problems that have become the preserve of the central state. The practice, approach and impact of such system leadership are the focus of the next section.

A framework of practice

The power for schools like Chalvedon and Barstable to federate was conferred by legislation in England in 2002 (DfES 2004). This allowed up to five schools to create a single governing body, pooled budgets and common management structure, effectively making one leadership group accountable for two or more schools. Such arrangements have become known as 'hard' federations. In practice, the legislation extended and formalized a range of existing pro-fessional practices, some of which were developed out of necessity by small rural village primary schools clubbing together to ensure survival while retaining their own autonomy. These looser structures have become known as 'soft' federations. The strength of the legislation is that it allows for a range of soft and hard federative forms to be developed in different contexts and to serve different purposes. The most common of these are raising students' attainment, innovating, and sharing resources and/or delivering curricular or welfare provision that one school alone cannot.

The focus here is on hard federations that seek to raise attainment in low-achieving schools. This usually occurs between a 'lead' school with a higher value-added score and a low performing 'partner' in need of support. We term these 'hard support federations' (after Potter 2005). Since the 2002 legislation, it has become gradually more common for such hard federations to be con-sidered as an effective means to support and renew low-achieving schools. There is little prescription, guidance or professional development on how these support federations should or could be most effectively undertaken. As such, executive headteachers, other senior leaders and governing bodies, often in conjunction with their local authority, have brokered, negotiated and developed their own locally-specific approaches. A range of models is being developed, yet, to date, there is only a small and emerging research literature (Potter 2005; Ainscow et al. 2005; Harris et al. 2006a; NCSL 2006; Higham and Hopkins 2007; Lindsay et al. 2007) and thus no well developed analysis on how hard support federations are being organized.

We analyse the key common practices and characteristics of six hard support federations. Four of these were between one lead and one partner school. One was between a lead and two partners. In the last, the lead had had three partner schools, two of which had recently migrated out of the support relationship. All the federations included only secondary schools. In most cases, the local authority had been a lead or supportive partner in working to help broker the federation as part of its own response to low attainment.

Each federation was committed to significant change in teaching practice and school ethos in the partner schools, based on a deeply held set of principles. These commonly included: a core belief that *every* pupil can achieve high standards; every pupil should be working towards explicit targets in each subject; every teacher should use assessment, diagnosis and data to inform planning and evaluate their impact on pupil performance; there should be an awareness of underperformance and clear improvement priorities, as well as a strong commitment to community involvement.

Perhaps the greatest challenge to achieving these improvements was the contexts in which rapid transformation was attempted. Not only was there usually a legacy of very low student attainment, low expectations and broader social deprivation; there was also not always agreement in the partner school that a federation was required and so pockets of palpable resentment could often be found. Such resistance appeared at odds with research findings that point to voluntarism, equality and open learning relationships as essential ingredients in successful school partnerships more generally (Arnold 2006; Spender 2006). However, in the sample we discuss here, there appeared to be (at least) four central aspects of a hard support federative approach that were significant in overcoming resistance and achieving improvement in the partner school(s) or, conversely, in the stalling of progress. These are set out in turn.

Lead schools

The internal capacity and capability for improvement within the lead school appear to be a prerequisite for success. Several points emerged. First, there was often a recent history of significant whole-school improvement in the lead school. In several cases, this had occurred in the same community or a similar socio-economic context to that of the partner school. This was a strength and lent greater credibility. In other cases, staff in the partner school were more likely to explain away the lead school's achievements in terms of higher prior student attainment rather than acknowledging the impacts of renewal in teaching, learning and school organization. This may be linked to more partner school staff starting to act as blockers to change. Second, the lead schools in many of the federations had developed a clear programme for their own school improvement with high quality learning environments and outcomes in a majority of departments and robust and effective management systems. Where this did not occur, progress in the partner appeared slow. For instance, in one case, a radically new model for renewal had been introduced across the federation as it evolved from a soft to a hard support structure under a new executive headteacher. The model focused on a project-based learning curriculum, widespread use of technology and large flexible learning spaces instead of classrooms. There was, therefore, less clear and proven expertise, practices or systems to export from the lead school or against which progress in the partner could be benchmarked. A variety of innovation occurred, but with mixed success. Third, nearly all the lead schools had had experience of working with and in other schools. Their staffs had gained experience of discussing and clarifying their own curricular and pedagogic strategies. Middle leaders were often capable of taking on coaching and mentoring roles. Senior leaders were skilled at managing boundary relationships, gaining and creatively deploying additional funding and organizing their own school to interface with others.

Leadership models

Each federation was characterized by a strong and resilient leadership team, a judgement emphasized by Ofsted inspections where these had recently taken place. In this context, two main senior leadership models had developed. In the first, as exemplified by Chalvedon and Barstable, the model was of an executive headteacher deeply involved in the day-to-day leadership of both schools and working in unison with an associate head based in the partner school. The associate role can best be described as a very senior deputy. This model was more common in federations between one lead and one partner. In the second model, the executive headteacher had taken on a more strategic and less operational role. Each school, including the lead, had appointed a head of school. The executive headteacher worked closely with each but behind the scenes, with one suggesting he would have failed if students started to identify him as their headteacher. This model was more common in federations of two or more partner schools.

Both models, however, shared several key characteristics. First, in every case, significant changes were made in the partner school's senior leadership team. There were no examples where the executive headteacher worked successfully with the original headteacher, who had either resigned or, less commonly, had agreed to move into a deputy's post in the lead school. Their replacement was often either a deputy from the lead school or an external senior leader known to and recruited by the executive head. Second, executive headteachers were clear that they were not 'super-heads' who achieved through their own skills alone. Instead, they sought to orchestrate the skills of others, drawing them into the decision-making process and, in doing so, building the capacity of others to take on wider leadership roles. Harris et al. (2006a) refer to this as the 'lateral expansion of existing leadership capabilities' with the executive headteacher taking responsibility for developing a distributed leadership team capable of transforming practice. However, importantly in our respondent schools, developing this capability often meant (at least initially) the colonization of a number of senior and middle management posts by lead school staff (either on promotion, secondment or both). This was seen as a quick and effective means to build and deploy trust and capacity in key posts of the partner school and to ensure a clear understanding of the approach to improvement and a commitment to its implementation.

Entry into the partner school

The preparation carried out immediately prior to and during the first months of the federation was seen by leadership respondents as being crucial in building strong federative foundations. There were two highlights. First, there needed to be a clear mandate and ground rules agreed by all key stakeholders, often in the form of a written contract. This was usually brokered by the local authority and included clear processes of accountability, improvement targets, governance arrangements, defined leadership autonomies and resources and, where appropriate, an end date and exit strategy. Bedding these down almost always took time, but nearly all the executive headteachers stressed the importance of being able to return to their mandate when the going got tough. Second, there was a need for diagnosis in the partner school. As Harris et al. (2006a: 404) have shown, partner schools frequently have detailed long-term plans but 'what is often missing is a clear link between self-review, action, impact and evaluation'. The new leadership team often instigated an immediate external inspection or more informal internal review to audit departmental strengths and weaknesses and benchmark future progress. Staff, student and parental surveys were often also undertaken. The findings, in conjunction with relevant national and comparative value-added data, were used to identify and target improvement strategies from across the federation. In a number of cases, this included the transfer of good practice from the partner school to the lead. Often, this was from one or two subject departments that had maintained good teaching strategies, curricular resources and student outcomes in spite of the overall school context. Where this did occur, it was often well publicized to partner school staff to emphasize the joint and 'objective' features of the approach.

The improvement process in the partner school(s)

In the heartland of the federative mission, there was inevitably a range of practices that constituted the actual improvement process in each different context. Extending the analysis in Chapter 2, we have found it useful to summarize the core common components of a federative improvement process with reference to Leithwood and Riehl's (2003) framework of three core leadership practices.

First, *setting direction* concerned building commitment to a federative vision of every learner reaching their potential. This was combined, in the partner schools, with a sense of real urgency, coupled with clear practical steps for change, usually focused on teaching and learning, curriculum and behaviour. The key leadership elements thus appeared to be:

- setting out a vision for a single direction in a complex organization to promote pupil entitlement and public accountability and demand high expectations for all students and from all staff;
- agreeing objectives and bringing immediacy to their delivery, with an action plan focused on termly improvements, use of evidence to tackle root causes of school weaknesses, and a sharp focus on pupil outcomes and the quality of learning and behaviour;
- establishing commitment to the federation and tackling early dissent and resistance by challenging the partner school's myths of adequacy or uniqueness, offering a way forward and securing quick wins to build confidence.

Second, *developing people*, which in the federations often included the introduction of 'standard operating procedures' in teaching and learning, against which partner school staff were held accountable and training needs were identified (with appropriate professional development provided through mentoring and coaching). Lead school staff often played a key role here by directly supporting the delivery of new practices, particularly in core subjects and in assessment for learning. Common leadership elements included:

- developing effective leadership and management, with an associate headteacher or the head of the partner school coached in both operational and strategic issues and an executive leadership team developed to be capable of transforming practice and outcomes;
- improving the quality of teaching, often with both a curriculum strategy and lesson plans imported from the lead school and lead school staff deployed to support implementation and coaching;
- building capacity, with staff working together to establish consistent practices and procedures, with, over time, partner school staff

coached in problem-solving skills and involved in more innovative work.

Third, *developing the organization*, which in these cases referred to implementing effective school systems to ensure reliability in approaches to behaviour, student tracking, pastoral care, staffing and timetabling (and that often replaced a reliance on a few individuals, Potter 2005). There was also a focus on improving the environment with an immediate clean-up campaign and the medium term upgrading of poor quality buildings. Core leadership tasks included:

- developing effective school systems and the use of data to evaluate success against benchmarks for improvement across a range of student outcomes;
- using excellence from the lead school, including, for instance, best practice in ICT, vocational education and so on;
- looking outwards to building supportive partnerships with primary schools, parents and the local authority, as well as wider community and business.

Knowledge transfer

Finally, throughout this work, the actual approach taken to put the lead school's knowledge and experience at the service of the partner school's improvement was important. In examining the more general transfer of good practice between schools in England, and as we saw in Chapter 4, Fielding et al. (2005: 72) argue that instead of 'transfer' the term 'joint practice development' should be used. Their argument is that this 'explicitly articulates a more learner-centred approach and provides a better description of what teachers aspired to and what they actually achieved together'. Their research also suggests that the '"transfer" model seems to be associated with delivery of "validated" packages of pre-formed practice seen by others to be good for the recipient' but which has 'little validity amongst teachers'. To a large extent, however, the transfer model appears to have a strong fit with the majority of federations in our sample. Moreover, the reality was often more nuanced than Fielding et al.'s dialectic. Indeed, as Potter (2005: 2) argues in the specific context of support federations, the 'principles and basic standard operating procedures are replicated' in the first stages of the federation, and 'more sophisticated elements of practice are co-constructed or customized' in later phases. Indeed, in several of our cases, a collaborative professional learning community was emerging in which lead and partner school staff worked collegially to establish new practices and innovations.

In this sense, the transfer of key elements of practice, such as management, behaviour, curriculum and teaching, might be best described as highly specified frameworks capable of being refined into context. To be effective, such refinement appeared to demand committed leadership, well resourced management, coaching in the partner school by lead school teachers and clear communication about the overall approach being pursued. In cases where these were lacking, problems emerged. For example, where leaders had not built a clear understanding that a range of practices would be replicated, middle leaders from the lead school reported frustration at having planned refinements that were never implemented and staff in the partner school reported feeling threatened and of working to preserve their own approaches.

A number of federative approaches also met with strategic or implementation difficulties or both of these across and beyond the four areas we have reviewed. Indeed, most of the executive headteachers stressed the importance of developing a culture of openness and trust that was, above all, blame-free so that lessons really could be learnt from problems and cul-de-sacs. Many of the federations were successful in achieving this professional learning ethos. In a small minority, the schools' original approaches remained dominant over a common federative drive and, as a result, trust and in some cases progress stalled. Given this range of experience, a broader question concerns the overall outcomes and benefits for students of federative working.

Outcomes and benefits

In reviewing the existing literature on executive headteachers and a range of federative forms, Glatter and Harvey (2006: 4) argue that the 'clearest conclusion to emerge for us is the paucity of evidence available'. The subsequent evaluation of the government's federation programme provided some additional evidence (Lindsay et al. 2007). The programme encompasses 37 federations – pilot-funded over three years – that vary across England in terms of size, purpose and (hard to soft) federative form.[3] The study found that nearly all the headteachers judged their federation to have been at least 'somewhat' successful in raising achievement over three years, but only a quarter suggested they had been 'very successful'. No statistically significant differences were found between federative schools in the programme and non-programme schools nationally in terms of pupil achievement at 11, 13 or 15 years old. At the widest measure of GCSE achievement (that of five A* to G grades), there was a higher percentage of pupils in programme schools, recorded as 93.6 per cent, compared to 91.3 per cent for non-programme schools. Unfortunately, in our specific case of hard support federations, two of the evaluation's three case studies declined to continue in the evaluation so that no cross-case conclusions could be made.

In many senses, therefore, the evidence-based jury is still out on federations. Further research is required and not only in terms of outcomes, but also more simply in terms of their overall number and distribution. As we argued in Chapter 2, currently there may already be more than one hundred federations of all forms in England.

In the sample reported on here, student attainment data was available for all the lead and partner schools as each had completed at least one full academic year within a federation. The impact on student attainment in each partner school at the benchmark of five A* to C grades at GCSE is set out in Figure 6.1 (in which the first entry for each school represents the year preceding the creation of a hard federation). This demonstrates an impressive trend towards significant improvement. In summary: eight out of nine partner schools had achieved improvements; in each case this had resulted in at least another 10 per cent of the student cohort reaching the GCSE benchmark; in many there had been almost a doubling of student achievement in the first year; in several, attainment had increased from under 20 per cent to over 50 per cent over a two or three year period. In addition, two partner schools had already finished their federative association with the same lead school and both had subsequently sustained student attainment. For instance, the highest achieving school in Figure 6.1 exited its federation after the 2005 results and sustained that level of attainment in both 2006 and 2007.

The only two partner schools not to raise student achievement were part of the same federation. In this case, however, a soft support federation had already existed during the previous two years (for which results are included in the graph in Figure 6.1). In this longer analysis, one partner had made significant progress while the other had not. The latter school – clearly identifiable as the lowest achiever in 2006 – in fact had avoided re-entering special measures in 2007. The judgement was based directly on the evidence the federation had been able to provide to Ofsted on both the level and focus of federative support and the predictions for progress that year. Both schools have subsequently become federative academies and so no results are available for 2007.

In the majority of the federations, these increases in student attainment were dovetailed with progress on student attendance, welfare and, where it had previously been of concern, behaviour (as reported by staff). Overall, for students, there was a strong sense that real renewal had taken or was taking place. These findings are consistent with two recent research reports that have a degree of interpretation on outcomes for students (NCSL 2005a; Potter 2005). Potter (2005: 1) reports that 'it is the firm belief of all interviewees that all schools, lead as well as partner, have made more rapid progress in federation than they would have alone'. The NCSL (2005a: 27) argues that the 'positive outcomes for the partner schools were very evident ... in terms of:

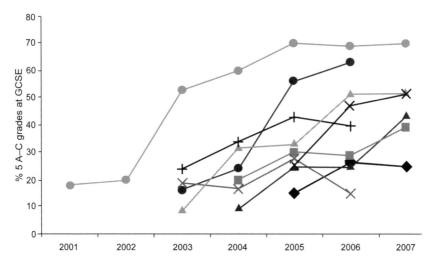

Figure 6.1   The percentage of partner school students achieving at the GCSE benchmark

Speed of transformation; ... Improved behaviour and attendance; A rigorous focus on learning and achievement; Enhanced school community confidence in the potential for the school to secure improvement'. It is recognized here that this chapter's sample displays the characteristics of mainly successful hard support federations. There is a need for further work to look for and at instances where federations have failed or dissolved. This may provide a different set of common characteristics, high on the list of which we may anticipate a lack of trust, communication and both distributed and system leadership capability.

Finally, standards of student attainment were sustained in each of the lead schools over the period of the federative leadership. This is demonstrated in Figure 6.2 in terms of the GCSE benchmark. Each school also sustained a contextually value-added score of above 1010. This is important given, as the NCSL (2005b: 4) argues, 'the demands on the lead school can be substantial [so] it is essential that it has the capacity to provide support without putting the education of its own pupils at risk'.

One may speculate that these schools, particularly those at lower levels of attainment, may have been better able to sustain their own progress off the plateau (as identified in Figure 6.2) if they had not been leading a hard support federation. This is a hypothetical argument about the opportunity cost of deploying their capacity for improvement elsewhere, for which there was some qualitative evidence. Conversely, the majority reported a range of professional development benefits for their own staff.

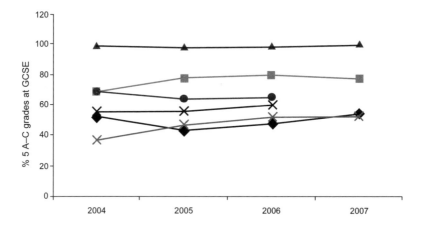

Figure 6.2 The percentage of lead school students achieving at the GCSE benchmark

Coda: implications for wider renewal

It is now widely agreed that very low-achieving schools, especially those in challenging circumstances, usually require external support to improve (Harris et al. 2006a). This is an argument given real clarity by Elmore's (2004: 253) research into what he says others call 'failing schools':

> Teachers were generally doing what they knew how to do, rather than doing what was necessary to produce the results they were trying to produce. In the absence of specific guidance . . . they would, other things being equal, continue to do what they regarded as 'good teaching'. In order to get different results, they would have to learn to do something they didn't know how to do, and in order to do that they would have to have access to skills and knowledge that would help them understand and enact those practices in their classroom. . . . The systems exhort schools and localities to provide support and professional development for schools in need of help, but don't actually invest in the infrastructure required to make sure that *that help gets to the right schools at the right time with the right technical expertise* (emphasis added).

The challenge Elmore presents is clear. Yet it is one that the dominant paradigm of state-led challenge and accountability, combined with (often) a postcode lottery of support, has never been adequately designed to fulfil. In this context, federations, developed appropriately to context, may offer a glimpse of a new methodology for tailoring professional expertise to specific local need. Certainly, the sample of hard support federations present here was, as a whole, already achieving deep and authentic renewal in teaching quality, institutional culture and student outcomes in contexts of historically low attainment and deprivation.

As has also been abundantly clear, hard support federations present exceptional challenges that requires strong executive and distributed external leadership and the wider capabilities and capacities of a lead school. This is system leadership in practice that takes responsibility for student outcomes across a number of schools and to do so:

- builds and mentors a wider and deeper leadership team;
- develops a collaborative organizational structure across two or more schools;
- transfers effective teaching practice and whole-school systems;
- widens student learning pathways and builds engagement;
- targets students at risk;
- recruits and retains staff across a wider career ladder;
- joins up with other children's services;
- brings professionals and communities together to work for social equity.

It is tempting to propose that the benefits of such system leadership should be enjoyed on a wider scale. But this aspiration raises several further issues.

First, the practice of system leadership across federations seems less likely to provide new solutions if it is prescribed or enforced. For instance, in the sample presented here, progress was often contextually negotiated, and where common characteristics did exist these would appear to demand significant refinement into other circumstances. This in turn would be predicated on professional decision-making to develop other fit-for-purpose federative models.

Second, proponents of a wider application of support federations (or similar approaches) must first identify a cadre of able, ready and willing leaders and lead schools. In the next chapter we go on to examine the emergence of National Leaders of Education, and their related National Support Schools, that might provide this cadre of 'change agents'.

Third, there would be complexities to manage. For instance, in conjunction with other new structures such as Educational Improvement Partnerships and Trusts, federations will create an increasing distance between the governance of some schools and the influence of local authorities (and hence local democratic accountability). It remains to be seen how strategic local leadership of both standards and equity can be assured across and between these increasingly independent groups of state schools. Yet this is vital, because it would be truly perverse to bring new meaning to the concept of a cycle of decline by replacing high and low achieving schools with a national system of high- and low-achieving federations.

It is important not to over-claim what is possible. We are reminded by Geoff Whitty (1997: 151) not to resort to 'false optimism, [by] exaggerating the extent to which local agency can challenge structural inequality'. Federations are not a panacea. The findings in this chapter, however, do point to the very real potential for federations to break local cycles of school decline. Where effective, they renew low value-added institutions while simultaneously demanding sustainable high standards in their lead partners. Above all, hard support federations are a means to improve the quality of leadership in pursuit of good teaching and learning.

7 Change agents of school transformation: consultant leaders, National Leaders of Education and their schools

The driving educational aim of the New Labour Government has been to raise the achievements of pupils and school standards. There has been 'no tolerance of failure'. No effort spared to urge schools to higher achievement in a culture of 'pressure and support'. And, to an extent, it has worked. Standards in primary schools improved quite rapidly for a time. Secondary school performance continued to inch up, although the widespread adoption of vocational GCSE courses complicates the interpretation of trends. From the turn of the millennium government ministers began to hail the success of their policies. But as always, schools in London were the subject of an uncomplimentary press.

The Schools Minister of the day, Estelle Morris, realized that there would be no unconditional success in improving education unless something was done about standards in London schools. This resulted in the government's introduction of the London Challenge, a unified range of strategies designed to 'banish failure' from London's schools. London Challenge advisers acted as the instruments of the government to diagnose the needs and broker support for schools failing to provide an adequate education. A key form of support was the attachment of a consultant leader to such schools. These were a new breed: heads of successful London schools, excellent leaders in their own right and committed to helping colleagues in other challenging schools. Increasingly, their own schools were drawn into this development role.

These early experiences have substantially informed the more recent introduction of 'National Leaders of Education' (NLEs). This chapter focuses on the emergence of NLEs in England who, together with their schools – termed 'National Support Schools' – now represent a strategic use of system leaders in the improvement of the country's most challenging or underperforming schools. The cadre of NLEs has grown from 68 in autumn 2006 to 180 two years later and will number 500 by 2010. Together with their schools, they epitomize system leadership in action. These NLEs exist both to make a difference to schools and to make an input to the development of national education policy. They provide a resource available to local authorities to use in transforming a school causing concern. They are working in consultant or executive leadership modes, particularly with National Challenge Schools, that is, schools in which too few students reach benchmark floor targets, and other challenged or struggling schools. As we have seen, NLEs did not emerge as speculative policy; they have their origins in a number of discrete initiatives, in particular the work of consultant leaders in London. We take this as our starting point in considering the emergence, deployment and impact of NLEs, first through a case study. Second, we consider the evidence of school progress and the impact of consultant leaders among other London Challenge initiatives. This leads, third, to an analysis of the appointment, deployment, work and impact of National Leaders of Education.

London Challenge: The London Leadership Strategy in action through the work of consultant leaders

The London Leadership Strategy is one component of the London Challenge initiative described in 'Investment for Reform' (DfES 2002b). It is led by the NCSL, working with other partners. The Strategy's rationale is that enhanced leadership capacity is a prerequisite for sustained school improvement and raising standards. This association is supported by the analysis of inspection evidence and research findings over many years (Leithwood and Reihl 2005; Matthews and Sammons 2005). There are two key partners within the framework of London Challenge. First, there are London Challenge Advisers, who identify the needs of underperforming schools and local authorities and either provide or commission the required support or intervention. Second, there are consultant leaders – mainly serving headteachers – who with their schools are assigned to work with underperforming schools to: build leadership capacity; help the leadership of those schools improve teaching and learning, and ultimately raise student achievement. How it works is best illustrated by a case study, one of many we have of consultant leaders working in London.

Monkswood[1] is a school that has been in and out of special measures for years. When the current headteacher was appointed to the school in 2005, the school was in special measures and virtually out of control. Students' behaviour was very challenging; the headteacher stated: 'It was not safe to walk the corridors'. The senior leadership was in disarray. There was incompetent teaching of English; no monitoring of teaching and learning, and no system of performance management. The curriculum was so limited as to induce disaffection, and there was a vast budget deficit as a result of a falling roll and financial mismanagement. The school was destined for closure. The school was under the microscope of the London Challenge Adviser, who arranged for an experienced headteacher and consultant leaders from elsewhere in London to act as mentors to the new head. Through the London Leadership Strategy, a Support Consultant (now a National Leader of Education) – who was headteacher of an excellent school in a neighbouring borough – was linked to the school and chaired the Board that was established to oversee the improvement of the school.

The new headteacher realized that he needed within a year to weed out incompetent teachers unwilling to change, establish a senior leadership team, develop curriculum leaders, improve teaching and learning and make major changes to the curriculum. The mentor, who became an accepted and regular visitor, focused on the senior leaders. One of the biggest challenges was to raise the standard of teaching. The support consultant's school, now a National Support School (NSS), provided the means of doing this. The NSS had become a 'teaching school' and a centre for intensive teacher development programmes to develop good and outstanding teachers. Over the following two years, most middle leaders from Monkswood attended the 'immersion' teaching and learning programme and some went on to undertake the 'outstanding teacher programme'. These courses provided nonjudgemental approaches to setting standards for good and outstanding teaching; practice in classroom observation and giving feedback; training in coaching; and the ongoing support of key staff. Middle leaders in the two schools were paired up; there was cross-school visiting and joint lesson planning and evaluation. The NSS made huge contributions to the teaching of subjects such as ICT, drama and media studies, and salvaged the crucial core subject of English. In short, the NLE and NSS, together with the consultant leader, whose periodic visits had continued for two years, helped the headteacher to put Monkswood on its feet. The local authority was also supportive in helping the headteacher to pursue the capability procedures which applied to three staff and the eight redundancies which the falling roll and financial deficit forced on the school. A new deputy headteacher had been appointed and the senior leaders were working as a team. All key staff knew their responsibilities and the school was beginning to attract additional students. Examination results were well above floor targets and rising. In 2008 the school was inspected again by Ofsted. From having had a statutory notice to improve, it was judged to be a 'good school', as shown in Table 7.1.

Table 7.1 Extracts from inspection reports for Monkswood prior to the headteacher's arrival in 2005 and three years later

Extracts from inspection report 2002	Extracts from inspection report 2008
Monkswood is a school with a few strengths but also a significant number of weaknesses... Pupils' attainment in Year 11 is well below average and pupils' achievements are unsatisfactory. Although the majority of pupils have positive attitudes to learning, the attitudes and behaviour of a significant minority of pupils are unsatisfactory – in some cases, poor. The quality of teaching is unsatisfactory in Years 7 to 11 and this is reflected in the quality of learning. Strategies to promote educational inclusion and equality of opportunity are unsatisfactory. Management is unsatisfactory overall with some strengths and a number of weaknesses. The school is not providing an acceptable standard of education and provides poor value for money. The sixth form provides a satisfactory education for its students and is cost effective.	Monkswood is now providing a good standard of education and care for its students. Managers, teachers and support staff, with strong support from the local authority, have worked extremely hard and with considerable success to improve those areas considered weak at the last inspection. The school is now on a much firmer footing and well placed to continue to improve. The headteacher, with the support of a talented senior team, has set a very clear direction for the school, with a determination to raise achievement and do the best for all students. They have insisted on raising expectations of what can be achieved and staff and students have risen to meet this challenge. Achievement is now good. National test results for 14-year-olds in 2007 rose considerably... Most students make good progress during their time in the school and develop good personal qualities.

The example shows the involvement of two system leaders in school transformation in a process which was commissioned and monitored by the London Challenge Adviser, representing the DCSF. Staff in the supporting school are very positive about the mutual benefits of the partnership, including the new skills, knowledge and understanding they gained professionally from working with colleagues in another school.

In the 16 partnerships studied, we have found that the use of consultant leaders has helped improve or transform leadership in almost all of the secondary schools with which they are linked. The data are complex because some of the secondary schools were being supported in the run up to closure, prior to being replaced by academies. Consultant leaders' influence is most effective when they work directly with the headteacher or headteacher and senior leadership team. Their impact is more diluted when they are asked to coach or train others in the school, such as middle managers (for whom other forms of provision are readily available) unless this is combined with work with senior leaders. In a few cases, work with middle leaders quickly provides a pathway to the headteacher. The mode of support is most commonly perceived as coaching, together with mentoring and facilitating. There are many examples in which the strength of relationships and level of trust result in frequent exchanges, not only through an often weekly visit but also by telephone and email, which can amount to an ongoing dialogue about the work of the school.

Particularly in highly challenging schools or those undergoing reorganization, the friendship, professional and moral support of a linked consultant leader is claimed to have made the critical difference between sinking and swimming for a headteacher facing unduly difficult issues. More generally, consultant leaders help the headteacher to focus on key issues amid a welter of demands, expectations and interventions. They undoubtedly provide a sounding board, but help the headteacher to filter, choose, decide and implement policies. Soon, however, purpose and direction must be introduced, encouraging the senior leaders to focus and act on priorities. As one consultant leader said:

> My approach has been to get to know the school very well and to listen, observing activities and discussions. I have encouraged the headteacher and colleagues to plan and prioritize the things that are most important and to use these as agendas for meetings. I have found it particularly useful to suggest regular review against these priorities. The main difficulty has been some of the senior staff who return to the same uncompleted tasks. I have, in these circumstances, been very specific about what I think they should achieve by next time.

Most consultant leaders also work with the senior leadership team, and some with middle leaders. Frequently, what starts out as mentoring, coaching or wider consultancy becomes a far-ranging commitment that draws in the consultant's own school as a resource. One consultant gives a flavour of this below, which also reflects our unequivocal findings that there is generally a reciprocity of benefits to the consultant leader's school as well as to the school with which the consultant is paired.

> A package, currently being put together, formalizes many aspects of our work. However, the headteacher has requested that I continue to act as a coach as she values our partnership. In addition, my school will be working on a number of school partnership issues to share expertise. For example, principals of core subjects from both schools will work on the 'immersion' teaching and learning programme together. One of her inexperienced deputies has been allocated time to shadow my curriculum deputy and work with our senior team in

order to experience good leadership practice and role models. We are a hub school for Assessment for Learning and have named her school as one of our partner schools for which funds have been allocated. All of this has been discussed and agreed with my governors, senior staff and staff. It is identified as a partnership and sharing of expertise between the two schools. We believe that we can learn a lot from them and that it will not be a one-sided learning experience.

Evidence of progress and impact

Conclusions about links between cause and effect must be tentative for three reasons. First, schools causing concern are influenced by such a range of interventions and initiatives that to identify the relative strengths of their contributions is difficult, as discussed by Matthews and Sammons (2004) in their evaluation of the impact of Ofsted's work. Second, the possible chain of influence stretches from consultancy work with the headteacher, to educational leadership at other levels in the school, and then to the influence of leadership on the quality of educational processes – particularly teaching and learning – before it affects the achievements of pupils, represented in part by higher standards. Similar problems have been described by Leithwood and Levin (2005) in discussing the way leadership may affect pupil outcomes. Third, it is easy to underestimate the school's own efforts, based on its staff's motivation and capacity to improve. The consultant leaders recognize this difficulty: 'It is early days to make really informed judgements. Achievement has risen, structures and priorities have been formulated and challenges have been shared. The school has moved forward and the principal has come through some difficult situations positively. I make no claims for me or my school in this but I feel we have helped confidence to grow and greater resilience to develop. Some of this is tangible but much is intuitive and comes from impressions on visits and in discussion.'

Other direct comments about impact show the consultants' recognition of the real goal. As one said: 'the school has come out of special measures. Exam data are showing improvement. I recognize the signs of an improving school,' and in another case: 'GCSE results improved over last two years. The school is out of special measures for the first time in a decade. Staff morale is higher.' The evaluator can look at the alignment of evidence. How much of it points in the same direction? Taking overall performance measures, there is evidence of differential improvement of 'keys to success' (underperforming) schools compared with all schools in London, and of London schools with schools elsewhere. The (Matthews et al. 2006: 7) evaluation, from which the quotations above are derived, drew a number of conclusions.

i. The quality of consultant leaders is central to the success and reputation of their work.

ii. The consultant leader programme overall is having a marked positive effect on school and leadership development in the schools studied.

iii. There are advantages in headteachers managing the consultant leader programme because of their own experience in London schools.

iv. Training in consultancy and coaching skills, with successful demonstration of their application, remains an essential prerequisite for this role.

v. Although all consultant leaders appear to have made an effective contribution to leadership development in the schools with which they work, their other priorities vary according to the circumstances of the school and inspection reports.

vi. The main strategies used by the consultant leader may be described as coaching and mentoring, followed by facilitating and counselling.

vii. The role of consultant leaders, and indeed the headteachers of the receiving schools, is complicated by the many forms of intervention and support that impinge on schools in challenging circumstances.

viii. The impact of consultant leaders is maximized where their own schools make a commitment and contribution to the partnership with the 'client' school.

Although it is difficult unequivocally to prove a causal link between the work of consultant leaders and improvements in quality and standards, qualitative (particularly) and quantitative findings all point towards a positive association. Consultant leaders work primarily to help to build and improve leadership capacity. This, in turn, is largely directed towards the quality assurance and improvement of teaching and learning so as to raise standards. Performance data suggest that higher standards ensue, and that consultant leaders make a contribution alongside other programmes. When taken alongside other London Challenge initiatives, the greater rate of improvement of London secondary schools compared with the country as a whole is clear (see Table 7.2). When launched in 2003, the ambitious objectives of the Challenge programme (DfES 2002c: 6) were to:

- raise standards across London secondary schools;
- re-establish London as a leading force in educational development;
- motivate in education professionals a desire to work in London;
- narrow the achievement gap within London's schools;
- provide highly effective models within the 14–19 and ECM agendas;
- grow a collaborative culture across London schools to enhance pupil learning;

- learn from London ideas, and disseminate the learning to others in England and internationally.

By 2008, many of these objectives had been accomplished. Ofsted (2006b) rated London schools as better, on average, than the rest of the country in terms of the schools' overall effectiveness, the quality of teaching, and leadership and management. Standards achieved by London's 16-year-olds were consistently higher than national averages for the first time ever (DCSF 2008b).

Table 7.2 Comparative performance between London and national students

Performance measures	London	National
In 2007 and for four years running London exceeds national averages in terms of the proportion of students achieving five or more GCSE grades A*–C in all subjects	60.9%	60.1%
In 2007 and for three years running London exceeds national averages in terms of the proportion of students achieving five or more GCSE grades A*–C including English and mathematics	47.9%	45.9%
Young people reaching level 2 (five or more GCSE grades A*–C in all subjects or equivalent) by age 19	74.1%	73.9%
Young people reaching level 1 (five or more GCSE grades A*–E in all subjects or equivalent) by age 19	50.5%	48%

London Challenge has provided a model for education intervention and support strategies in other cities from Bristol to Manchester, all of which have incorporated the appointment of consultant leaders to lever systemic improvement in those areas. The turnover of staff in many London schools has been radically reduced. The number of secondary schools in special measures, that is, failing to provide 'an acceptable standard of education', has been reduced from 40 to three. A proliferation of extended schools (see Chapter 5) is providing out-of-hours education and care, together with other services. Consortia of schools and colleges ('collaboratives') are making progress with the 14–19 curriculum and accreditation reforms and the extent of inter-school collaboration in London has grown markedly.

The role and appointment of NLEs

The concept of NLEs emerged in a government White Paper (DfES 2005a) in which the Secretary of State asked the NCSL to identify a group of National Leaders of Education – outstanding leaders (in primary, secondary or special schools) – who not only demonstrated excellent leadership in their own school but would also be able to support schools in challenging circumstances, particularly those in special measures. In a letter to all headteachers in England (NCSL 2006: 1), Steve Munby, Chief Executive of the National College for School Leadership, described the NLE role and invited headteachers who met the criteria to apply. The NCSL sought school leaders who,

> currently lead high capacity schools and who, with their school, can provide leadership and capacity thus enabling a school to come out of special measures. We are looking to identify some of our very best leaders who have the skill to go into a different and challenging context, to provide leadership and who are also able to bring with them, as appropriate, a range of other support and expertise from their existing school.

It was envisaged that the first tranche of NLEs would be in the region of 50. These leaders would also have access to Ministers to advise on education policy and have responsibility for helping to grow future NLEs. To be successful, the NCSL indicated (Munby 2006: 2) that NLEs would first need to meet the following criteria:

- have extensive evidence of successful school leadership, achieving sustained high standards and significant added value;
- be a leader in a school that was judged in its most recent Ofsted inspection as having at least very good or outstanding leadership and management;
- have a strong track record of providing effective support to other schools in difficulties;
- have current experience in leading a school which can demonstrate: consistent high performance; strong senior and middle level leadership; a range of staff at all levels with coaching and mentoring skills, and experience of helping other schools in difficulties.

Second, NLEs should also reflect important personal characteristics. For example, they should be:

- articulate and reflective about improving schools in difficulties;

- committed to taking responsibility for schools other than their own;
- absolutely determined to improve outcomes for children and young people;
- able to inspire and energize;
- expert in managing and sustaining change;
- strategic and flexible in tackling challenges; and
- have a deep understanding of the teaching and learning process.

A third condition was that staff in the NLE's school would need to be well placed to take on what was termed 'this additional opportunity', since the school would need to be designated a National Support School. Designated NLEs and their National Support Schools would then be a national resource, available to local authorities.

Nearly 300 of the 24,000 headteachers in England (1.25 per cent) responded to this invitation. A first group of 68 were appointed after a rigorous selection process (Matthews 2006b) which included reference to their own school's performance data, references, inspection reports and, in about half the cases, visits to the schools. National Leaders of Education represented maintained schools of all types and sizes. There have been three further recruitment rounds in response to the government's intention to increase the number of NLEs to 500 by 2010. By December 2008, there were approximately 200 NLEs.

Characteristics of NLEs

Headteachers appointed as NLEs were, without exception, successful, capable and committed school leaders. Almost all had worked with other schools or headteachers, particularly as mentors to new headteachers, national strategy consultants, consultant leaders or Leading Edge partners (see Chapter 4). They were held in high regard by their colleagues, who – in those schools visited – were remarkably consistent in describing their qualities. A study of the first group of NLEs (Matthews 2007: 21) found several compelling and largely common characteristics:

i. They show strong and principled moral purpose in reaching out to help other schools, sharing what they have learned, from highly credible foundations.
ii. They are motivated by the challenge of providing the best possible educational experience for young people.
iii. They are thoughtful and systematic in the way they work, diagnosing the challenges and finding workable solutions.
iv. They earn the trust they receive through consulting, valuing and

developing the people with whom they work, and having belief in them.

v.   They build confidence, capability and self-esteem in the people with whom they work, as well as institutional capacity through growing other leaders.

vi.   They have inordinately high expectations, great optimism and believe in success. Nothing less than excellence is good enough for them.

vii.   Problems that would daunt many headteachers are diminished by them.

viii.   They are decisive and prepared to take unpalatable decisions if this is the way to provide what children and the community deserve from their school.

ix.   They are admired and respected by their colleagues, providing excellent role models.

x.   They will find innovative and often unorthodox solutions to both systemic and more localized problems; and will not always follow expected patterns and rules.

In practical terms, NLEs and their schools place great emphasis on monitoring and improving the quality of teaching and learning and on using formative assessment, and focusing on both to track and accelerate learning. They distribute responsibility and accountability to a range of leaders in the school, and give huge priority to continuous professional development, which commands a significant proportion of the budget.

These characteristics are not confined to NLEs, but it is an endorsement of the process through which the first NLEs were identified that they are so strongly reflected across the group. Similar characteristics can be seen in other effective system leaders, including, for example, consultant leaders working within the London Leadership Strategy element of the London Challenge. They are found in headteachers breaking new ground in extended or full-service schools, leading federations and leading successful schools in very challenging, often urban, circumstances. The characteristics also provide a model to which less experienced or effective headteachers can aspire. They do not need to be system leaders to exhibit such attributes, but the confidence and commitment to lead in such a manner may take time to develop. It is, though, worth noting that within these leaders' schools and elsewhere there are far greater numbers of staff, particularly advanced skills teachers, coordinators and heads of department, and members of senior leadership teams, who are working with their counterparts in very different schools. This takes the same commitment and courage. There was considerable enthusiasm among the staff interviewed for the prospect of becoming recognized as a National Support School.

Deployment of NLEs

National Leaders of Education are intended first and foremost as a resource on which local authorities can draw if they have a school in difficulty, commissioning the services of the NLE and their school, the National Support School, to help another out of its difficulties. Increasingly, the assistance or intervention is a contractual one, particularly if the 'client' school has a breakdown in leadership. Typically, when an NLE is approached to work with a school in this way, the NLE will wish to visit the school and consider the size and scope of the job to be done. Often, the NLE will then arrange to conduct a 'due diligence' examination of the school to enable the work to be specified and a price determined on the basis of the staff and other resources that will be needed to turn the school around. This forms the basis of a contract between the local authority or, sometimes, the governors of the client school, as commissioner, and the governing body of the National Support School as provider.

Models of deployment of NLEs and their schools

About a third of NLEs in 2008 were deployed in executive headship roles, carrying responsibility for the leadership of a school in addition to their own. The majority act in a range of supportive roles without carrying executive responsibility. These roles include school-focused consultancy, coaching, mentoring and associate headship, as well as wider system leadership roles concerned with leading school support strategies or acting as support consultants to consultant headteachers or local leaders. The NLEs who discharge these roles have two things in common: they all remain practising headteachers, usually leading National Support Schools which are outstanding, and they all have the skills to undertake a variety of 'system leader' roles. The main roles are summarized in the right hand column of Table 7.3.

System director and support consultants

There are, of course, important system leadership roles at national and subnational levels in terms of school support and improvement. From its inception in 2003, the London Leadership Strategy (LLS) has been led by a London secondary headteacher, *primus inter pares*. The current Director is an NLE, seconded half-time from his secondary school to lead the provision of pan-London leadership development opportunities. The role as he has developed it includes:

Table 7.3 Tabulation of the roles of NLEs and others

Leadership *in situ*	Examples of school characteristics	Requirement	System leader *or other agent*
Region or city-wide leadership of school support, improvement and development of system	Leads and manages the delivery of school improvement strategies involving a range of consultancy and other provision	Acute strategic vision and system leadership skills	**System director** **Support consultants working across an area**
Community or complex leadership	Federation of schools or extended provision	Executive responsibility across providers	**Community or executive headteacher (established)**
Dysfunctional leadership	School that is failing its pupils or regressing (a 'red' school)	Decisive action and assumption of control or responsibility	**Executive headteacher (NLE)** (takes over the leadership of the school for a period)
Challenged leadership	School in challenging or changing circumstances; headteacher with good potential; weaknesses in leadership team; results perhaps below floor targets at Key Stage 2 or Key Stage 4 (National Challenge School)	Support for the headteacher in building leadership capacity and attention to quality so as to transform the school	**Consultant leader**
Transitional leadership	School with an acting headteacher undergoing reorganization	Support based on similar experience	Associate headteacher
Inexperienced leadership	Scope for improvement and a need for change	Advice, support and coaching for the headteacher	*Headteacher mentor/ coach*
New headship	School not causing concern	Mentoring in the role	*Headteacher mentor/ coach*
Leadership requiring challenge	Coasting	Challenge	*School Improvement Partner*
All schools	Any	Challenge, support and monitoring	*School Improvement Partner*

- responsibility for the recruitment, training, deployment, monitoring, support and development of tens of consultant leaders (some of whom are NLEs) working in the primary and secondary sectors and pupil referral units in London, and the quality assurance of this work;
- the incubation, development, piloting and roll-out of new types of professional development provision which systematically support such key objectives as raising the quality of teaching and learning through focused, school-based training for improving teachers, good teachers who want to become outstanding, excellent and advanced skills teachers, and so on;
- making a strong contribution to national policy including the extension of London Challenge and innovations such as the establishment of the first four 'teaching schools' in the capital;
- ensuring that his school remains not only outstanding – as one of the handful to have been deemed outstanding (or previously very good/ excellent) in four successive inspections – but strives to improve on the previous best.

Area-wide leadership of school support, improvement and development system

A second example of managerial system leadership is represented by the LLS support consultants, several of whom are NLEs. Their role is to broker the partnership between consultant leaders and the schools they support, provide any necessary mentoring or coaching for the consultant leaders, monitor the progress of the school and the effectiveness of the partnership and act together with the Director as a management group for the Strategy. Support consultants are often well placed to chair partnership boards which bring together the key players concerned with supporting the improvement of a school in an Ofsted category.

Executive headteacher (established)

Increasingly, NLEs are being appointed who are already executive headteachers of (usually) two schools in a soft or hard federation. In other cases, what starts out as an NLE deployment to a nearby school as temporary executive (see below) headteacher evolves into a permanent arrangement as the schools become linked through a federation or trust. These permanent or established executive headships are not considered further here (having been discussed in detail in Chapter 6).

Executive headteacher (NLE)

Most NLE executive headteachers take over responsibility when leadership is in crisis. The headteacher may have left, be absent on health grounds or be clinging on. It is usually very difficult if there is a weak head in post, owing to the incumbent's resistance to anyone else taking over, but these things have a way of resolving themselves. If there is a new head or one with potential, a neo-federation approach can work. In the most commonly encountered and favourable scenario, there is no headteacher in post in the school requiring help. This allows the NLE some flexibility in proposing appropriate arrangements. Three typical scenarios are:

- to become acting head of the supported school for a period, leaving the NSS deputy head to take responsibility for the home school on a day-to-day basis as acting or associate head;
- to identify an acting head of the supported school, either from within the staff or to second one of the NSS senior leadership team (usually a deputy head) to lead the supported school under the guidance and mentorship of the NLE as executive head, using the vacant post in the NSS school for leadership development; or
- to work with a new 'head of school' in the supported school in a type of federated arrangement.

Consultant leader

The majority of NLEs fall into this broad category. The role of consultant leader has been described as 'helping the heads of other schools to develop leadership capacity and improve teaching and learning so as to make their schools more effective'. They act as consultants and as brokers of other services to the school. Everything they do has the ultimate aim of improving outcomes for learners. The consultancy role has three closely related elements: coach, mentor and facilitator, working with the headteacher and, often, the senior leadership team and middle leaders as described earlier.

Evidence of the relative impact of these different roles and a large body of knowledge about bringing schools out of special measures suggests that, where leadership is dysfunctional in a school, replacing it brings about the quickest and clearest results. A growing proportion of NLEs find themselves in executive headship roles. Consultant leaders can achieve a considerable amount when working with a receptive head and senior leadership who have the potential to become effective. National Leaders' of Education work is best regarded as covering a spectrum of approaches to intervention and support which can be tailored to achieve the most rapid and sustained (through capacity-building) results in a particular case.

> We worked with a school in special measures. I work alongside the head and his leadership team supporting them in a variety of ways, for example, with subject reviews, capability procedures, coaching and mentoring senior staff, sharing policies, etc. In November 2007, we held our first joint professional development event which was very successful. Four of my middle leaders and my deputy head have been involved in learning partnerships with subject leaders. My staff work alongside their colleagues by sharing good practice, especially schemes of work, lesson planning and joint observations. My deputy head has taken part in subject reviews with me and has also led a review of assessment across the client school. We have been very pleased with the success of our partnership and were delighted when the school came out of special measures after we had been working with them for 8 months.
>
> (An NLE, interview, Spring 2006)

The benefits for system leading schools are often as tangible as for supported schools. As the NLE in the example above stated: 'For the duration of the partnership, there were huge benefits on both sides; my staff learnt a great deal from their visits, especially in terms of behaviour management. Their staff said that they gained a lot from sharing systems and approaches to teaching and learning.'

The impact of NLEs

It has quickly become apparent that NLEs and NSSs provide leadership and oversight of school improvement that ensure actions are identified, taken and evaluated. Inaction is not an option for a school. This is a different level of intervention from the coaching, consultancy or mentoring role of consultant leadership, notwithstanding the fact that NLEs will draw on all these approaches where they are appropriate. The NCSL (2008: 3, original emphasis) is right in asserting that

> there is widespread agreement that it is well-led schools that improve schools. Rigorously constructed, robustly implemented and closely monitored plans for improvement have been shown time and again to provide the battle plans for remedial and improvement action. As yet, effective ways of *ensuring* that improvement takes place in the most underperforming schools have not been established. In particular, where the challenges are significant, where leadership is less than good and/or where there is insufficient capacity, schools are especially in need of a secure route to improvement.

National Leaders of Education can provide this route. They have now amassed a significant track record of bringing schools out of special measures, improving schools with 'notices to improve', helping re-establish strong leadership in schools that lack it and stabilizing fragile or turbulent schools. The NCSL (2008: 3) produced some headline figures in terms of NLEs' contribution to raising achievement:

> Over 30,000 pupils in struggling schools have now received support from more than 120 National Leaders of Education and National Support Schools during 2007. Data and Ofsted monitoring and inspection reports are highlighting the progress that schools are making and the impact NLEs are having. NLEs are able to help move schools out of special measures within 9 to 10 months on average. In supported primary schools in 2006–07, there has been a 6.4 per cent increase in the percentage of pupils achieving level 4 or better in English SATS, and a 5.0 per cent in the percentage of pupils achieving level 4 or better in Maths SATS results for the schools supported. This compares with little year on year change nationally. In secondary schools, client schools supported by National Leaders for at least six months improved the percentage of pupils achieving 5 or more A*–C grades by 3.9 per cent (a relative increase of 11 per cent). This is a substantial level of improvement which would be sufficient in many cases to raise outcomes above floor levels in underperforming schools.

These improvements were often achieved in a very short time (under a year) and, given more time and deployments, improvements will be even more impressive. Hill and Matthews (2008: 30) have examined validated data for 2007/08 and unvalidated 2008 results for all the schools that were either phase 1 NSSs or were supported by phase 1 NLEs/NSSs, where the results were available at the time of publication. In interpreting the data they pointed out that:

- not all the effect, whether positive or negative, is necessarily due to NLEs and NSSs;
- the nature of NLEs' interventions varies from consultancy to executive control, making it difficult to generalize about a generic effect;
- all schools in Ofsted categories are subject to focused school improvement efforts of various kinds. At this stage it has not been possible to assess the added value of NLEs by benchmarking their impact against that of a 'control group' of schools supported by non-NLE means, but as the programme grows this option should be explored;

most schools experience some fluctuation in results from year to year. The smaller the year group, the greater the effect of a small group of pupils on overall results.

Despite these caveats Figure 7.1 does show that in most cases NLE involvement is associated with improvement in the client school being supported, and with continuing improvement in the NSSs. This holds good in both the primary and secondary sectors. The real test, however, will be demonstrating sustainable improvement over the longer term.

Analysis of the results of secondary schools supported by the first tranche of NLEs, appointed in autumn 2006 and deployed during the 2006/07 school year, shows that there was a pattern of improvement in both the headline figure of five or more passes at GCSE grades A* to C including English and mathematics and overall. The improvement becomes most apparent between 2007 and 2008 (Figure 7.1a). Equally, it is crucial that the improvement of an underachieving school is not at the expense of the supporting school. Figure

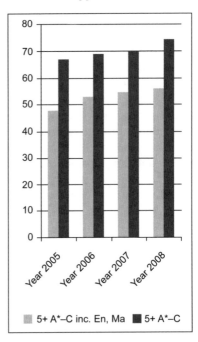

Figure 7.1   Overall average percentage of pupils achieving five A*–Cs grades at GCSE (with and without English and mathematics) and five or more A*–C passes overall (assuming that schools have the same cohort sizes)

7.1b shows the trend in results of NLEs' school during the same period. The data corroborate a wealth of evidence that suggest that school to school improvement partnerships are mutually beneficial.

The trends in results illustrated in Figure 7.1 obscure of course the progress of individual schools. The actual results of the 17 supported secondary schools over four years are therefore shown in Figure 7.2. While there is a great deal still to be achieved in these schools, half of them recorded gains of nine percentage points or more in terms of the proportion of pupils achieving five good GCSEs – and in some cases the increases were dramatic. In other schools the 2008 results resulted in more modest increases but marked the reversal of a downward trend or the consolidation of an upward one. Results fell back in just two schools. The patterns of improvement are similar in supported primary schools and primary national Support Schools.

The data, together with Ofsted reports which cite the effect of NLEs and case studies, provide accumulating evidence of the impact of the NLE/NSS initiative. The real test will be how well schools have developed the leadership capacity to sustain improvement once the NLE withdraws. Longitudinal monitoring of the progress of supported schools will provide the necessary evidence.

Coda: towards the future – NLEs and consultant leaders as change agents

National Leaders of Education reflect our earlier definition of school system leadership (Chapter 1) in its entirety. The government has accepted that extending the NLE programme will have a significant effect on reducing the number of schools causing concern, particularly those failing to reach floor targets. It could also lead to more federations, trusts or other clusters of schools under the leadership of exceptional headteachers, in tandem with NSSs. We are also seeing the expansion of executive headships in the primary sector where NLEs are increasingly being asked to oversee other schools in 'soft' federations. Cross-phase work will also continue to be encouraged where appropriate. Currently, there are examples of secondary school NLEs working in primary and special schools, special school NLEs in secondary schools and primary NLEs in secondary schools. The NCSL, which oversees the NLE provision, expects that other leaders will support schools in challenging circumstances at the lighter-touch end of the spectrum as consultant leaders, leaders of groups of Local Leaders of Education and interim headteachers. In this way, NLEs will contribute to improvement across the system and play a broader transformative role in addition to highly targeted and intensive support for the schools most in need.

A comment attributed to Sam Stringfield is that the United States is

Percentage of 5 A*–C GCSE passes including English and mathematics

Percentage of 5 A*–C grade GCSE passes overall

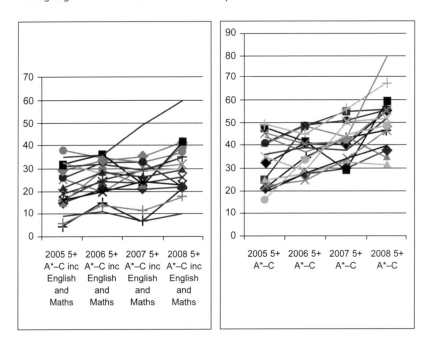

Figure 7.2   Change in results from 2005 to 2008 in 17 secondary schools partnered by NLEs

perpetually awash in 'new' and self-proclaimed 'highly effective' programmes for improving students' academic achievement. In terms of novelty, the NLE programme is best regarded as a strategic initiative which harnesses the best of the developments which preceded it, particularly the use of consultant leaders in London. This effectively road-tested the system leading principle of professionals helping professionals and schools helping schools. The NLE programme is best regarded as an example of government – through the NCSL – endorsing, harnessing and moving to scale the lessons learned from London Challenge. Turning to Stringfield's second challenge, can we say that the NLE programme is highly effective in improving schools and raising achievement? There is certainly evidence that NLEs help schools improve. Their deployment has been a key instrument in pulling a growing number of schools out of Ofsted categories. In more schools than not, there is growing evidence of an association with raising standards. This suggests that NLEs are also the most likely agents to raise the standards of National Challenge Schools above floor targets, and the decision to expand their ranks is well justified. National

Leaders' of Education are highly effective at turning schools around, but the real test of effectiveness is whether those schools are left with the capacity to sustain their improvement, to move from satisfactory to good and beyond, and to put standards on a sustained upward trajectory. It is too early to say, but the signs are good. The programme is making a major contribution to leadership development and succession planning. National Leaders' of Education deputies are being blooded as heads of schools and are being appointed to the headships of the schools they have supported. Other leaders are rising through the ranks to take their place. The value of these supplementary benefits is considerable.

Evaluation in progress of the work of NLEs suggests that:

- they have well developed and reliable systems, procedures, expectations and operating standards in their own schools which are sufficiently robust to sustain the quality, efficiency and effectiveness of the school's work despite perturbations in staffing or other factors, and sufficiently tolerant to permit initiative and innovation;
- these systems and practices are operated with a high degree of consistency;
- there is effective devolved leadership working to common principles and procedures;
- staff training and development have a high priority;
- systems, procedures and practices are largely transferable or adaptable to other schools and contexts.

The identification of NLEs and NSSs and evaluation of their work and impact offer the opportunity to capture definitively the practices that work best in transforming schools and sustaining their effectiveness. The increasing body of evidence of the impact of their work suggests that headteachers working as system leaders with other schools may provide the best lever we have for helping ineffective schools to become good schools.

8 The prospects for system leadership

The form and character of school leadership described and analysed in the preceding chapters hold the key to system transformation. This is a bold statement and one that we do not make lightly. By temperament and discipline, we tend to avoid grand claims, particularly given the over-use of words such as 'transformation'. But here we claim, on the basis of the evidence presented in this book, that it is warranted. Our dictionary defines transformation as 'to change completely the appearance or character of something or someone, especially so that they are improved'. This, we suggest, is close to the picture we have been painting in earlier chapters of what widespread system leadership could achieve in the English education system. The emerging landscape is both radically different from what goes before but also makes so much sense that it may soon become commonplace.

Our recent review of school leadership in England for the Organisation for Economic Co-operation and Development (OECD; Higham et al. 2007) set out the broad forces having an impact on school leaders since the mid-1980s, the specific challenges these created and the ways in which school leaders, and the education system more generally, have responded. We also noted a very clear narrative about the way in which school leadership in England has evolved during this time that is consistent with the argument of this book. This is as follows:

- The somewhat *laissez-faire* and paternalistic culture of leadership in the 1980s changed radically as a direct consequence of the introduction of Local Management of Schools (LMS) in the Education Reform Act (1988) that allowed all schools to be taken out of the direct financial control of local authorities.
- By devolving resource allocation and priorities from local authorities to governors, headteachers *de facto* became considerably more autonomous. This autonomy, however, was tempered by the highly developed national framework that held them accountable for school performance and subject to significant areas of national prescription.
- The publication of examination results and a national inspection regime where reports on individual schools became publicly available put considerable pressure on headteachers and served to

encourage the high degree of competitiveness among schools in the mid-1990s.

- This competitive environment was mitigated somewhat by a growing commitment to collaboration, for which a wide range of government initiatives such as Excellence in Cities, the Leadership Incentive Grant and Primary Networks provided incentives. This trend was enhanced by the establishment of the NCSL and the increasing professionalism with which school leadership was being regarded.
- The New Relationship with Schools was a further attempt by the government to develop a more mature balance between the centre and the front line and to streamline accountability and bureaucratic processes to ensure a more personalized education for students.
- Inevitably, the policy challenges for school leaders have increased dramatically over this period. Two critical and current examples are the balance between standards and welfare and the impetus for school diversity and parental choice.
- But, whatever the general and specific challenges of policy implementation, the ability to work and lead beyond an individual school is of increasing importance. It is estimated that nearly all schools in England are involved in some form of collaborative activity or networking.
- This, in turn, is leading to a more collaborative approach to schooling: school leaders are having a significantly more substantive engagement with other schools in order to bring about school improvement that leads to system transformation. This system leadership, which we have seen in detail in this book, is where school leaders, in a variety of roles, play an active and explicit role in system reform.

Since the mid-1980s there has been a remarkable movement from schooling as a 'secret garden' to significantly increased levels of accountability and autonomy that led to overt competition. This is now rapidly being replaced by sophisticated forms of collaboration that are leading to a transformation of the landscape of school education, all in the pursuit of higher standards of student learning, welfare and achievement. And it is the school leader who is increasingly in the vanguard of this movement. It is this accumulation of events that appears to be leading us inexorably towards a transformational moment, where dominant forms of top-down control can be replaced by more lateral forms of accountability and support. It is, as Gladwell (2002) would say, a potential 'tipping point'.

Such moments, though, are distinguished not just by the accumulation of a series of linear events but also by a broadening and deepening of the substantive agenda. Documenting this complexity has been our task in this book. The description of the historical context and the empirically-based chapters lead us to six key themes that summarize this potential transformational moment. Whether they are powerful enough to take us over the tipping point remains to be seen, but they are worthy of comment in a concluding chapter. They are:

- the primacy of leadership;
- the emergence of system leadership;
- the transfer of innovation;
- the new educational landscape;
- policy implications for educational transformation;
- the systemic imperative.

The primacy of leadership

It is clear from the evidence of this book and other research that effective leadership is central to school and system transformation. We have argued that the destination is a 'new professionalism' and that (system) leadership is the way to get there. Teaching, learning and well-being must be the unrelenting focus of reform. A new professionalism, by which we imply leadership at all levels, will lead a renewal and deepening of the teaching and learning process and will engage students more authentically in doing so. Leadership of learning, within and across schools (that is, system leadership), is the new lever needed to build capacity for this progressive change. The emphasis on leadership across schools is important not only because of the moral commitment to children and young people more widely but also because of the knowledge and expertise it brings in: a symbiotic relationship, perhaps, each furthering the other.

To support this argument, we will draw here on two additional sources of evidence from the 'Impact of Leadership on Pupil Outcomes' project in which some of us have been involved. The first is a substantial review of the international literature on the relationship between school leadership and student achievement. This has resulted in a number of publications, the most accessible of which is *Seven Strong Claims about School Leadership* (Leithwood et al. 2006). Space precludes a detailed discussion of these 'claims', but four points can be highlighted from this international evidence that complement the evidence in this book and support its argument:

- First, leadership provides the facilitating conditions for school transformation. In this sense, leadership is indirect, the means to the end rather than the end itself.
- Second, the core practices of leadership are broadly applicable across

contexts and cultures, although, of course, they have to be adapted to circumstances and, critically, they have this singular focus on creating the conditions for improving the quality of learning, welfare and achievement. This is the leadership of teaching and learning. We discussed this point in some detail in Chapter 2 and examples to support it are presented throughout the book.

- Third, leadership is a function that, to be fully effective, needs to be distributed within the school. There is no tension in our minds between notions of 'distributed' and 'system' leadership: they are simply the different faces of the same coin. As has been argued consistently in earlier chapters, system leadership cannot possibly exist without a sophisticated approach to distributed leadership at the school level and even the inter-school level.

- Fourth, there are the personal qualities of the leader. We highlighted this point first in the model of system leadership introduced in Chapter 2 and it has been an implicit theme thereafter. Simply put, system leaders may well be charismatic individuals, particularly at the early stages, but the critical personality traits are those to do with caring, resilience, persistence and optimism.

This international evidence provides support for our perspective on the primacy of leadership. It endorses the characteristics and qualities that we have been finding from the research reported here. Yet as helpful as it is, this emerging knowledge base on leadership still lacks a 'theory of action'. This is something that we have also been paying attention to in the 'Impact of Leadership on Pupil Outcomes' project. It is still work in progress but a critical path seems to be emerging that is captured in Figure 8.1 (Hopkins 2007b).

In the figure the action flows from left to right. The first important factor is the leader him or herself whose potential contribution to school transformation appears to be determined by an interacting set of characteristics and experiences. These are then focused by the context of the school and the leader's ability to respond to a wide variety of contextual factors. The leadership function is exercised on the four basic practices associated with student learning discussed in Chapter 2. These create within the school an enabling infrastructure that produces the conditions for higher levels of student learning outcomes. We now have emerging empirical evidence to support this critical path (Day et al. forthcoming). The value of such an analysis is that it gives a sense of direction to leadership practice that, hitherto, has remained largely implicit.

The processes at the heart of this evolving model are well illustrated by several of the outstanding schools led by NLEs. Both the NLE and their schools aspire to be world class and see constant improvement of current practice as the key to this. In terms of building vision, for example, Outwood

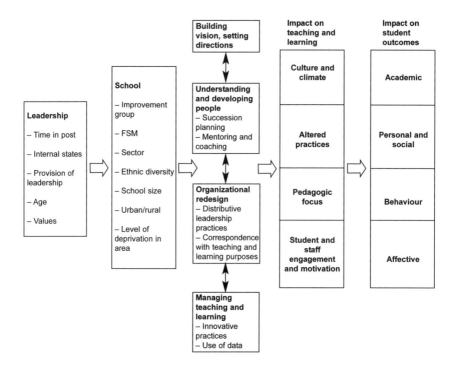

Figure 8.1   Connecting headteacher effectiveness and pupil outcomes

Grange School, Wakefield – one of the largest in the country – knows that improving on current best practice is the way to sustain excellence. Its *vision* is expressed through seven key areas of development ranging from 'lessons for learning' to 'training for growth', always with the avowed purpose of putting students first. *Understanding and developing people*, in this context, includes opportunities for staff to commit themselves to a range of professional and leadership development. Emerging leaders are challenged by engagement in one of the development areas of 'deep support' and 'deep learning' (concepts drawn from the work of David Hargreaves), each led by a vice-principal. As a training and teaching school, the school is a provider of training through its 'Transforming Middle Leaders Programme', marketed to other schools; succession planning is enhanced through its provision of wider experience for leaders in supporting schools with which the college is partnered. *Organizational redesign* is a constant process of evolution. In one glimpse of the school, students were being consulted about reorganizing tutorials as vertical or cross-age groups; the curriculum was being redesigned and work was progressing towards forming a trust with neighbouring schools. *Managing teaching and learning* is at the heart of raising performance, with teaching levels – from inadequate to outstanding – being clearly defined. The commitment to students is that their lessons will have a consistent pattern, using five stages; they will know how to get better; they will enjoy challenge and support; and they will take responsibility for their own learning. The enrichment of learning and use of data for pupil tracking are highly refined processes.

The emergence of system leadership

The argument should now be clear that system leadership tends to emerge as a natural consequence of involvement in school improvement efforts, that, as leaders improve and transform their own schools, they learn much about the process and are motivated to share this knowledge with other schools. We exemplified this in Chapter 3. It represents a radical shift from the competitive ethos of the 1990s and towards a degree of altruism that has always been latent in the profession.

In Chapter 1 we outlined the policy context that actually makes the system leadership role absolutely necessary. As national systems of education move towards increasing decentralization, the responsibility of leadership to contribute to system renewal and transformation becomes all the more important. We documented in subsequent chapters the variety of roles that system leaders are taking in England at present.

There is not, however, as we saw in Chapter 1, a seamless transition from National Prescription to Schools Leading Reform. We are certainly not claiming that the journey is complete: we may be moving towards Schools Leading Reform, but we are by no means there yet. We have already noted a number of barriers to achieving this, but one in particular needs to be revisited here. We discussed, in the introduction, the emergence of system leadership and also commented on the 'system management' critique. In Chapter 2, we claimed that our evidence showed that system leadership could be thought of as an emerging professional 'movement', rather than as an elite practice of a few 'super-heads'. We also noted a significant distinction between headteachers undertaking roles created on a *national* scale, predominantly within the ambit of government-led programmes, and those taking on roles developed at a *local* level as a result of their personal commitment to system-level change.

There is a fundamentally important point emerging here. There are some who claim that system leadership is just a cynical government ploy to exert increasing control over the system – in other words, as a barrier to rather than as a facilitator of system transformation. The argument of this book and the evidence we produce to support it suggest that there is a good deal of agency on the part of the system leaders. Most of our examples show leaders in a positive and progressive light as agents of reform and transformation rather than as upholders of the *status quo*. Certainly there are instances where the design of national system leadership roles or the implementation of them by individual leaders relates more to system management. But this may be an important role to play as the system moves itself from vertical to horizontal ways of working.

It is important, therefore, not to polarize positions too early in the debate and to see such roles and functions as 'either–or'. In fact, we see this far more as a spectrum or continuum with a number of overlapping roles. It may be helpful to use a typology to differentiate types of leaders/schools in the current system. On the basis of our current evidence, we can identify at least three broad categories of role that roughly relate to three phases of the transformational process: a) system managing, b) system partnership working, and c) system leading. While there will always be a need for each of the three categories in any system, their relative importance will vary from phase to phase of development. We have illustrated this in Figure 8.2.

The three categories of role are as follows:

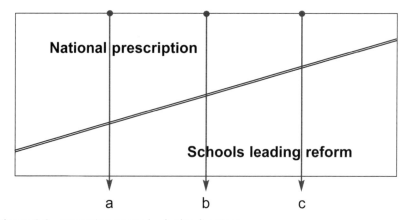

Figure 8.2 Integrating system leadership functions

a) *System managing* refers to nationally developed, funded and administered leadership roles, regarded by some as only extensions of the state's prescriptive arm. We do not adopt this position. We see these roles as necessary in any system and also as harbingers of a whole-scale approach to schools leading reform. The point is that as the system changes such roles, while still necessary, will become less numerous and important. Some of the best examples of this role, as mentioned in this book, are the SIP and the early use of consultant leaders in the Primary National Strategy. Parenthetically, it is instructive to note that the SIP role was designed as an archetypical system leadership role. Some of us were involved in the original policy work on the SIP and are somewhat disappointed at how the initial conception has been distorted towards vertical accountability through the process of implementation.

b) *System partnership working* is defined as seeking collaboration as a spur to improving one's own provision, to developing capacity for doing so and then sharing this with others. We regard this as a transitional phase leading to more radical and transformational forms of inter-action. We have seen, for example in Chapter 5, how the concept of community education has become overlain with a strong agenda for children and young people as a result of the Children Act. This means that schools, increasingly, are partners in a network of cross-agency providers seeking to make integrated arrangements for edu-cation, care and other aspects of well-being. The challenge here is for leadership within a partnership (rather than leadership of a part-nership) of unequal but essential players within local systems so that the needs of all individuals are met and their interests safeguarded.

c) *System leading* refers to having the expertise, credibility and capacity to lead learner-centred (local) system change while sustaining one's own school. It is important to stress that other players are at work here in addition to system leadership headteachers or principals, for example, those having an outreach commitment in the system lea-ders' schools. Several chapters have given substance to this theme, showing how school headteachers and their colleagues are effective in leading the transformation of their schools and others. It points to a future in which school trusts, federations and networks, working with unified and distributive leadership structures provide not only the means of delivery but the answer to challenges of improvement, sustainability, social justice, leadership development and succession planning. What is important in this view of system leadership is that it never loses sight of the core purpose of the school: to provide for high quality teaching, learning and care. The emergence of NLEs and, importantly, the designation of their schools as NSSs are among other examples we have discussed in the book.

If genuine transformation is to occur, then the forms of system leadership described in this book will need to become dominant, but there will always need to be a variety of roles, particularly during times of transition. This discussion of roles and the emergence of system leadership – as important as it is – should not disguise the essential nature of the transactions that system leaders engage in. This is the focus of the following section.

The transfer of innovation

At the heart of the examples from our research is an implicit process of innovation transfer: how does one school codify the practices that have been critical to its own success and then enable them to be transferred to other schools as key building blocks for improvement? Let us look at three perspectives on how to transfer innovation. The underlying point is that system leaders, like other change agents, trade in powerful ideas that can transform the life chances of others. In the context of system leadership, these are the theories in action related to the curriculum, teaching, learning and assessment that create the conditions within which virtually all young people can learn.

Many have become excited recently over the potential of 'viral communication' as an approach to managing and implementing educational change. Viewing this process as akin to the spreading of a virus contrasts starkly with the recent dominant model that sees change move from the centre to the periphery.

We have already referred to the best known exposition of this alternative theory of change – Malcolm Gladwell (2002) in his book *The Tipping Point*. He argues that every successful innovation that has an impact on society has a 'tipping point' where the change transforms itself exponentially from enjoying a limited local or sectional interest to become a mass phenomenon. In detailing this process, he identifies three laws of the 'tipping point' that have a particular relevance for system leaders.

- The 'Law of the Few' says that resources for viral communication ought to be concentrated on those who are responsible for starting word-of-mouth epidemics. In a social epidemic, as in system leadership, these are the core roles and skills for spreading a movement.
- The second law of the 'tipping point' relates to the 'Stickiness Factor'. This suggests that there are specific ways of making a contagious message memorable; relatively simple changes in the presentation and structuring of information can make a big difference to how much of an impact it makes.
- The third law of the 'tipping point' is the 'Power of Context'. This says that human beings are a lot more sensitive to their environment than they may seem. That is why social change is so volatile and so often inexplicable.

Gladwell argues that there is difficulty and volatility in the world of the tipping point, much as there is in the world of system leadership. He also claims, and as we have seen in previous chapters, that there is a large measure of hopefulness as well. We have good evidence in previous chapters of system leaders who are good at building alliances, presenting powerful ideas accessibly and being acutely sensitive to how these ideas are enacted in differing contexts, all reflections of Gladwell's three laws. In the end, we agree with Gladwell when he says that tipping points are a reaffirmation of the potential for change and the power of intelligent action; so, we would claim, is system leadership.

The second perspective is provided by David Hargreaves (2003) in his monograph *Education Epidemic* where, working within the same paradigm, he outlined an agenda for educational transformation based on innovation and networking. The essential task, Hargreaves argued, is to create a climate in which it is possible for teachers to engage actively in innovation and to transfer validated innovations rapidly within their school and into other schools. This does not mean a return to 'letting a thousand flowers bloom' but a disciplined approach to innovation.

If Leading Edge schools – by definition a minority – take the lead in knowledge creation, he asks, what happens to innovation in the rest of the system? Hargreaves responds that transformation is achieved in two ways:

- by moving the best schools (or departments within them) further ahead. That is, through *front-line innovation*, conducted by Leading Edge institutions and government supported 'pathfinders', which develops new ideas into original practices; and
- by closing the gap between the least and most effective schools (or subject departments) – *transferred innovation*.

Transformation thus combines 'moving ahead' with 'levelling up'. To achieve such a 'lateral strategy' for transferred innovation requires the following strategic components:

- It must become clear what is meant by 'good' and 'best' practice among teachers.
- There needs to be a method of locating good practice and sound innovations.
- Innovations must be ones that bring real advantages to teachers.
- Methods of transferring innovation effectively have to be devised.

Networks, Hargreaves argues, are the foundations for an innovative system of education. Only networks can deliver a mix of vertical-central and lateral-local reform strategies necessary for transformation. In short, the system itself has to become a more self-conscious and effective learning system in parallel to the learning organization advocated for schools.

The third perspective is linked to Michael Fielding's and colleagues

(2005) notion of 'co-production' that we have referred to earlier. We have seen in a number of examples from our research that, by working collaboratively, schools can co-design and share practice, as with LEPP in Chapter 4, and develop new forms of community provision, as seen in Chapter 5. Co-production does not stand in contrast with the two previous perspectives but is a complement to it. It is an issue of 'both/and' rather than 'either/or'. As is seen in the following section, the key point is context. Transfer and refinement will be appropriate in some contexts; co-production more appropriate in others. Both seem to be part of the broader methodology of system leadership. The collaborative point is very interesting. For example, we have some new evidence relating to the provision of integrated services and the 'challenge of being a leader within a partnership' (of equals). This is reflected in the need for schools not to dominate the leadership of integrated children's service provision in an area. Where is the system leadership here? It can be a cooperative approach.

We are clear that the ability to transfer proven practice from one school to another is a key component of system leadership and that there is, as we have just discussed, increasing clarity about how to do this. The question of how we move this to scale remains a key issue. It is to a discussion of the new educational landscape that we now turn.

The new educational landscape

The argument in the preceding section leads inevitably to a consideration of what a new educational landscape that espouses lateral rather than vertical and hierarchical forms of relationship would look like. The key point here is that different forms of intervention and mutual support are being provided increasingly by schools themselves, rather than being imposed and delivered by some external agency. This depends critically on excellent practice being developed, shared, demonstrated and adopted across and between schools. Further, this implies school-to-school support as the basis for the implementation of differential improvement strategies.

There are three aspects to the new landscape that we will consider in this section: first, a framework for thinking about highly differentiated improvement strategies and how they can promote more lateral ways of working; second, some examples of how this framework can move to scale; and, third a consideration of the system leadership roles involved.

It has been clear for some time that schools at different stages of development require different strategies, not only to enhance their capacity for development but also to provide a more effective education for their students. Strategies for school development need to fit the 'growth state' or culture of the particular school. As Gray et al. (1999) argued, strategies that are effective for improving performance at one 'growth state' are not necessarily effective at another. We need to move beyond a 'one size fits all' approach that has traditionally characterized much external support and become better at providing responsive improvement strategies to particular growth states.

An example of how such differential support is already taking shape across the education system is set out in Table 8.1. In the left hand column is a simplified categorization of school type based on Ofsted's categories. In the second column is an example of the improvement strategies that may be most appropriate for each school type. The important point here is not only that these strategies are customized for schools in a particular growth state but also that they are provided by other schools rather than an external agency. Also, in most cases, these strategies create a virtuous circle of collaboration insofar as they provide an improvement activity for the leading school as well. It is mutual support – or what the Specialist Schools and Academies Trust calls the 'by schools for schools' approach – that is the basis

Table 8.1 System leadership roles and highly differentiated improvement strategies

Type of school	Key strategies – responsive to context and need	System leadership roles (top)/system working (middle)/system support received (bottom)
Outstanding schools: leading schools	• Become curriculum and pedagogic innovators • Support lower performing schools	• Lead an innovation partnership • Network extended provision • Consultant leader • Executive headteacher • National Support School (NSS)
Good schools: effective but with internal variation	• Regular local networking • Subject specialist support to other schools	• Member of education improvement partnership • Or an innovation partnership to move from good to great
Satisfactory schools: under-performing schools	• Supported as a linked school • Consistency interventions	• Partner school in improvement network (e.g. SSAT) • Support by consultant and local leaders of education
Inadequate schools: failing their pupils	• Formal support in a federation structure • New provider	• Support by NLE and NSS • School sponsored academy

of the movement away from top-down external intervention and towards an educational landscape characterized by reciprocity and lateral ways of working. The right hand column lists some of the system leadership roles that actively promote this way of working.

As we have already made clear, the analysis of system leadership roles suggests that, to achieve transformation, such leadership will need to be expressed at a variety of levels within the system, in particular at the national, local and school levels. We summarize this reapportioning of roles as follows:

- *System leadership at the national level* – with social justice, moral purpose and a commitment to the success of every learner providing the focus for transformation and collaboration system-wide;
- *System leadership at the local level* – with practical principles widely shared and used as a basis for local collaboration and transfer; and with specific programmes developed for groups most at risk;
- *System leadership at the school level* – with, in essence, as we have seen in this book, school leaders becoming almost as concerned about the success of other schools as they are about their own and, as a consequence, having an increasing impact on the governing levels of the whole system itself.

In this section we have been describing the various system leadership roles necessary to achieve system transformation. We turn in the following section to a consideration of the policy context necessary for this to occur.

Policy implications for educational transformation

It is clear that the practice of system leadership will bring new challenges and roles for school leaders and their schools. What is less clear is what this might mean for other system actors, most notably the government. If school leaders are to take on wider responsibilities for system reform, how should the government work to develop such activity? And would a real and authentic commitment by the government to do so inevitably mean a rebalancing of roles, agency and control between it and schools?

As we have seen, fundamental elements of system leadership are the more authentic collaboration on and transfer of school improvement intelligence and best practice in leadership by experienced leaders. These are inherently professionally led, bottom-up solutions. But they are solutions to problems that have traditionally been the responsibility and preserve of the central apparatus of the state. This includes the deeply ingrained workings of the accountability, funding and governance systems that place the unit of an individual school at their centre. In considering this tension it is worth briefly returning to the division identified in Chapter 2 between system leaders working in national programmes and those working in locally organized, often ad hoc, roles. As demonstrated, many system leaders operate in national programmes that have created incentives for activity through organization, funding and professional development; these, in turn, have created new opportunities for headteachers and other school leaders. This is the 'enabling state' at work. It is an important step towards rebalancing agency by making it more possible for school leaders to lead solutions in a widening professional domain of cross-school and system improvement.

Yet, within these opportunities, we may already be witnessing limitations of government-led activity. For, while new leadership roles emerge, the government's tendency to check and control does not seem to diminish significantly. This tendency is related to a focus on effectiveness and value for money. But it also seems to portray a government that is still yet to develop sufficient trust in the profession. The result is less than 'intelligent' accountability and, at the extreme, a tick-box bureaucracy, rather than dynamic system reform. The evidence is word of mouth but mounting. We already hear concerns about the accountability functions SIPs are being asked to perform and how this restricts the time they have available to engage in conversations that provide professional support and challenge. We also hear mutterings about schools joining consortia or loose co-federations primarily because this is where they feel the government will place funding or access to future initiatives and programmes.

There are, of course, variations to this bottom-up, top-down dialectic; we have already argued against this polarization and for a continuum or spectrum of overlapping roles. Some centrally driven momentum is needed, but on the principle that system leadership must inherently be a professionally led agenda. Furthermore, from this perspective, the role of an 'enabling state' becomes focused on reducing barriers to collaboration and wider policy disincentives, with national agencies providing bespoke professional development to individual system leaders.

How these (and other) possibilities may inform current professional action and government influence will depend on a range of criteria. If, however, a shared criterion is to develop effective system leadership in a growing number of schools, then the following suggestions for more short-term action may prove instructive.

- *Suggestion 1: provide incentives rather than legislate.* The traditional response has been intervention and management from government, national agencies or local authorities. A more lateral approach may be to create the conditions within the system to promote system leadership and collaborative activity, for example, through adjusting accountability requirements, and funding for capacity-building.

With the right incentives, schools will naturally move towards these new ways of working and mould them to their contexts and challenges.

- *Suggestion 2: place the agency close to the school.* In England, there are now at least three emerging change agent roles within the system – consultant or local leaders, NLEs and SIPs – whose remit is specifically school improvement. The intention that must be maintained is that, instead of creating a new bureaucracy, their brief is increasingly focused on facilitating relationships among schools to maximize purposeful collaboration.
- *Suggestion 3: use school 'independence' collaboratively to tackle underperformance.* Recent moves to give greater independence to state schools and free them from excessive bureaucracy are important. But it is using this independence to work collaboratively that is a particularly appropriate organizational format for schools, especially those in the inner cities, where rapid transformation of standards and support for students is most needed.
- *Suggestion 4: listen more to the views of leading professionals*, who are experienced at making policy meaningful in different contexts. We have shown that governing by initiative and short-term fix is counter-productive to sustainable improvement. As system leaders take more responsibility and control of educational change, government will, as Hargreaves (2007) argues, need to be more willing to openly debate and find agreement with professionals on the moral purpose of education.

What is striking about these proposals is that the influence of the state is markedly reduced. This, however, is not an argument for an extreme form of devolution. It is simply a recognition that, as a system becomes more competent, the role of the state inevitably changes. To further this analysis, we stand back a little in the next section from system reform in English education and locate our argument in the evolution of change in public services more generally and again more broadly in wider international efforts for school reform. We draw on recent advances in the thinking on public sector reform, on our work with leading principals around the world and what international leadership studies say about the systemic importance of school leadership.

The systemic imperative

The push for educational reform in England since 1997 has been part of a more general attempt to reform public services. It is interesting to place the emergence of system leadership within this context. A Cabinet Office paper (2008) entitled *Excellence and Fairness: Achieving World Class Public Services* is illustrative. Here a radically different approach to reform is proposed as a way of moving the UK's public services towards becoming world class. Being world class, the Cabinet Office argues, involves achieving excellent outcomes, offering personalized approaches, being fair and equitable, and offering good value for money. It acknowledges that persisting with too many top-down targets can be counter-productive and that too much centralized government control will stifle local initiative. A new approach is advocated that emphasizes empowering citizens, a new professionalism and strategic leadership. Although the argument is inevitably detailed, it is worth reviewing it briefly here, as there is a strong connection to the themes of this book.

The emphasis on *citizen empowerment* refers not to choice, but to the requirement to focus public services on the needs of those who use them rather than those who provide them. It is also about citizens having the power to work collaboratively with services rather than passively receiving them. The read-across to education and the themes of this book are clear. In our context, this reflects the shift in focus from teaching to learning, the encouragement of 'student voice' and well-being, and the creation in the school of powerful contexts for learning.

The focus on *new professionalism* ensures that innovation, consistency, continuous self-improvement and responsiveness are driven from within the public services themselves. This requires that, once core standards are reached, services need to unleash the creativity of those who work on the front line. Again, the similarity to the themes of this book is striking. System leaders, on the evidence presented in this book, develop knowledge and theories of action about how best to support the learning and achievement of their students, respond directly to their needs and innovate from a platform of consistently high quality.

There is still a role, though, for governments to provide *strategic leadership*. Although the role has changed from one of command and control, world-class public services depend on governments providing leadership by setting a clear vision, a stable framework, adequate resources, effective incentives as well as accessible and consistent information on performance. Only governments can take this broad view and, although it means rejecting micro-management, it does not imply the *laissez-faire* that provides no direction, standards or vision. This strategic and enabling role of government is precisely the one we have been advocating for system leadership.

These are not three disconnected elements but are linked together in a dynamic relationship that renews (or reforms) the public sector. This reflects the types of interactions and relationships we have been advocating in this chapter for the continuing development of system leadership. In this way, ideas emanating from the centre of government about a broader agenda for social policy reform appear to support the further emergence and development of system leadership.

This may also have a wider appeal to international developments in educational change. Recently, many nations, both developing and developed, have engaged in massive reform efforts to better their education systems and practices. Generally speaking, many of these are intended to ensure that schooling is more effective and efficient in preparing and educating *all* citizens for the rapidly extending global economy. Interestingly, many of the policies and strategies practised by one country can rapidly become the targets of reform for other countries. This is what some commentators have referred to as the 'policy epidemic'. This also provides some evidence of a global policy agenda that is narrowing its focus on a small number of key drivers such as the personalization of learning, increasing the quality of teaching, using the pressure for accountability more formatively, and placing increased emphasis on the role of the school (and networks of schools) in making the journey towards widespread improvement (Hopkins 2007c).

To enable a global dialogue among education leaders on these themes, and to initiate an international network of innovative leadership, 100 outstanding headteachers from 14 different countries (known colloquially as the G100) were recently invited by iNet[1] to participate in a workshop in Beijing in October 2006. During the three-day workshop, in which one of us was involved, the headteachers discussed their experiences and views of education reforms in their own schools and education systems. They were clear that leadership must be a central piece of the global policy jigsaw. Not only do the many reform efforts aimed at transforming schools – new governance frameworks, more accountability, and more decentralization – require leadership to shoulder the greatest responsibilities and to bear the most direct consequences. These people are also central to the eventual outcomes of any reform efforts.

At the end of the workshop, the headteachers prepared a communiqué that expressed their vision for the global future of schooling. They claimed that there should be a global sense of moral purpose in education. They defined moral purpose as a compelling drive to do right for and by students, serving them through professional behaviours that improve quality while also increasing equity and, through doing so, demonstrate an intent to learn with and from each other. In this way, the workshop illustrates that the emergence of system leadership in England may not be an isolated phenomenon.

This view is supported by evidence from the OECD's recent project on school leadership. The project sought to provide policy-makers with analysis to help formulate leadership policies capable of improving teaching and learning. One of the studies on 'School Leadership for Systemic Improvement', in which one of us was again involved, argued that in seeking to prepare young people with the knowledge and skills needed in a rapidly changing world the roles and expectations for school leaders have changed radically. 'They are no longer expected to be merely good managers but leaders of schools as learning organizations. Effective school leadership is increasingly viewed as key to large-scale education reform and to improved educational outcomes' (Pont et al. 2008: 6).

A key area recommended for further research was 'system improvement', which the study defined as school leaders taking responsibility for contributing to the success of other schools as well as to their own; or where regional or local teams engage leaders in working collaboratively to support one another in achieving common goals of student learning. The study found that the practice of such leadership in England is among the most developed in the OECD. It was also noted that this had been publicly developed and supported in England in recent years. England, the study concluded, provides a strong example of how headteachers and principals are shouldering wider 'system roles' to share capacity and intelligence for the whole system's benefit.

Coda: the prospects for system leadership

The evidence cited in the previous section helps locate the prospects for system leadership within a broader context. It supports our claim that system leadership, as we have described it in this book, is not an isolated activity engaged in by a few idiosyncratic 'hero innovators'. Rather, it has the characteristics of an emerging movement focused on the one hand on achieving as high a level of learning for individual students as possible and social justice on the other.

Such a movement is pursuing a systemic agenda. Our dictionary defines the system as 'a complex whole, a set of connected things or parts, organized bodies of material or immaterial things'. We were heartened by this definition. For us it captures precisely our intention for adopting the phrase 'system leadership' when, at around the start of the new century, we recognized a change in attitude and behaviour on the part of our leading headteachers. It was not simply a set of behaviours focused on short-term change but was an attempt, confident in what had been achieved in the recent past, to reach for a future that was firmly grounded in equity, potential and social justice. Few articulated their actions in such terms but the implicit assumptions were clear to see. The phrase 'immaterial things' in the dictionary definition is important, too. It is about changing a culture of expectations and ways of working that have held our system of education back for far too long, but there is still a way to go.

The evidence of this book is convincing; much can be achieved through the forms of collaborative activity we have documented. This is not an antigovernment agenda. Government, both national and local, always has a role to play. But the nature of this role will change as the level of competence within the system increases. It is now relatively clear what national governments have to do to move an education system from low to adequate levels of performance. This is part of the policy epidemic referred to earlier. The crucial point, however, is this: as a system moves to adequate levels of performance, further increases cannot simply be mandated. Reform of a strikingly different quality is required. To misquote a recent and profound saying – governments can mandate adequate levels of performance but the move from good to great has to be 'unleashed'. It is only by achieving this rebalancing and, we believe, by harnessing the combined creativity and skill of professionals and schools that high levels of quality and fairness can be achieved.

As Paulo Freire, the great Brazilian, once put it: 'No one educates anyone else. Nor do we educate ourselves. We educate one another in communion. In the context of living in this world.'

This is what system leadership in practice is all about.

Notes

Chapter 1

1 The concept of a 'national system, locally administered' was central to the 1944 Education Act and, as Chitty (2002) argues, integral to the broader post-war settlement.

2 The sources for both Tables 1.1 and 1.2 are: Glatter (2003); Vangen and Huxham (2003); Rudd et al. (2004); Ainscow and West (2006); Arnold (2006); Connolly and James (2006); Spender (2006); Cordingley and Bell (2007); O'Leary and Craig (2007); Stevenson (2007).

3 For instance, headteacher respondents to research commissioned by the National Union of Teachers identified '58 types of externally-imposed initiatives [during their headship], but were hard put to think of any tasks that had been taken away from them other than those they had delegated' (Smithers and Robinson 2007: 31).

4 Other examples include, first, the Social Partnership, comprising most school workforce unions and associations, which now works with the government on workforce remodelling, including on measures designed to tackle the workload and excessive working hours of teachers and headteachers. Second, there are the new experimental efforts by national agencies to construct their dissemination approach collaboratively with professionals so as to 'secure ownership, genuine implementation and sustainability' (Cordingley and Bell 2007: 6).

5 Carole Whitty was until recently Deputy General Secretary of the National Association of Head Teachers.

Chapter 2

1 Special Measures is the formal improvement category in which schools in England are placed by Ofsted if they are deemed to be failing to provide an acceptable standard of education. A school in Special Measures will be inspected regularly by Ofsted to monitor improvement. One category less in terms of the severity of inspection judgement and response is when a school is given a notice to improve because it is performing less well than could be reasonably expected.

2 These included the National College for School Leadership (NCSL), Ofsted,

Specialist Schools and Academies Trust (SSAT), Association of School and College Leaders (ASCL) and National Association of Head Teachers (NAHT).

3   There may be some overlap where leaders are undertaking multiple roles.

4   This represents the number of Leading Edge partnerships in England. The exact number of system leaders is more complex as there may well be more than one in each partnership. This is explored in Chapter 4.

5   This consists of numbers as of October 2008 including: London 68; Manchester 46 (including those awaiting training); and Black Country 20 (as an estimate).

6   This is at October 2008; it is intended to increase to 500 by 2011.

7   The overall total of 1313 is substantially lower than the 3078 we proposed in Hopkins and Higham (2007). Having further developed our theory of system leadership, we have now excluded over 2000 Primary Strategy Consultant Leaders (PSCL) from the 'Consultant Leaders' section. This is because PSCLs only supported the implementation of the external Primary Strategy rather than leading whole school improvement and drawing upon their own schools in the process of doing so.

Chapter 3

1   The actual school names have been changed to protect confidentiality.

2   Ofsted changed its definitions of what constitutes satisfactory, good or better teaching during this period, but not to a degree that would significantly alter the data quoted for the school.

Chapter 4

1   Ebbutt (1985: 156) describes action research as: 'the systematic study of attempts to improve educational practice by groups of participants, by means of their own practical actions and by means of their own reflections upon the effects of those actions'.

2   McKernan (1996) proposes a similar but more detailed cycle of: define problem, needs assessment, hypothesize ideas, develop action plan, implement plan, evaluate action, decisions (reflect, explain, understand action).

3   In their own self-evaluation, many schools recognized that they were not well developed across all these criteria. In particular, a whole-school culture of sharing effective practice was often least developed.

4   As Ofsted (2003: 35) argues, 'it is no longer true – if it ever was – that leadership and management are the sole responsibility of the headteacher. High quality leadership and management must be developed throughout a school's

organisation if new challenges, many of which require working much more closely in partnership with other schools and agencies, are to be met.'

Chapter 5

1   Facilitated by the National College for School Leadership.
2   Sure Start is the government programme to deliver the best start in life for every child. It brings together early education, health, childcare and family support, often based in Children's Centres.
3   Not to be confused with Community (as distinct from Foundation) schools.
4   'Connexions' is a service which offers advice on education, careers, housing, money, health and relationships for 13–19-year-olds in the UK.

Chapter 6

1   Until September 2005, 'serious weaknesses' was one category less in terms of the severity of inspection judgement than special measures. Since 2005, a school in this category is now judged to require significant improvement and is therefore given a 'notice to improve'.
2   The federative model is common among primary schools in the Netherlands. There are currently around 7,000 primary schools in the Netherlands, of which 80 per cent (5,600) have one governing board for two or more schools. On average, these federations comprise 11 schools, with 237 staff members and 2,471 pupils (NCSL 2006).
3   The 37 federations receive varying levels of government funding amounting to £16 million overall. Half contain schools that are 'in Ofsted categories, low-attaining or under-performing' (NAO 2006).

Chapter 7

1   A fictitious name is used here for reasons of confidentiality.

Chapter 8

1   iNet is the international arm of the Specialist Schools and Academies Trust. Its published aim is to be an international network of schools and academic organizations that have committed themselves to achieving significant, systematic and sustained change through networking and the sharing of innovation to ensure the best possible outcomes for all students in all settings.

iNet organized the workshop with the support of the Hong Kong Foundation and in collaboration with China's National Academy of Education Administration.

References

Ainscow, M. and West, M. (2006) Drawing out the lessons: leadership and collaboration, in M. Ainscow and M. West (eds) *Improving Urban Schools*. Maidenhead: Open University Press.

Aitchison, J. (1995) School management in the market place: a secondary school perspective, in A. Macbeth, D. McCreath and J. Aitchison (eds) *Collaborate or Compete? Educational Partnerships in a Market Economy*. London: The Falmer Press.

Andreae, J. and Matthews, P. (2006) Evaluating the quality and standards of early years education and care, in G. Pugh and B. Duffy (eds) *Contemporary Issues in the Early Years: Working Collaboratively for Children*, 4th edn. London: Sage.

Arnold, R. (2006) *Schools in Collaboration: Federations, Collegiates and Partnerships*. EMIE, Report 86. Slough: National Foundation for Educational Research.

Ball, S. (2003) The teacher's soul and the terrors of performativity, *Journal of Educational Policy*, 18(2): 215–28.

Bentley, T. (2003) Foreword, in D. Hargreaves, *Education Epidemic: Transforming Secondary Schools Through Innovation Networks*. London: DEMOS.

Brighton and Hove Council (2006) *Children and Young People's Business Plan 2006–2009*. Brighton: Brighton and Hove Council.

Cabinet Office (2008) *Excellence and Fairness: Achieving World Class Public Services*. London: Cabinet Office.

Campbell, D., Coldicott, T. and Kinsella, K. (1994) *Systemic Work with Organizations: A New Model for Managers and Change Agents*. London: Karnac Books.

Chitty, C. (2002) *Understanding Schools and Schooling*. London: Routledge.

Coffield, F. (2007) *Public Sector Reform: Principles for Improving the Education System*. London: Institute of Education.

Coleman, A. (2006) *Collaborative Leadership in Extended Schools: Leading in a Multiagency Environment*. Nottingham: NCSL.

Collarbone, P. and West-Burnham, J. (2008) *Understanding Systems Leadership: Securing Excellence and Equity in Education*. London: Network Continuum.

Connolly, M. and James, C. (2006) Collaboration for school improvement: a resources dependency and institutional framework of analysis, *Educational Management, Administration and Leadership*, 34(1): 69–87.

Cordingley, P. and Bell, M. (2007) *Transferring Learning and Taking Innovation to Scale*. Nottingham: Innovation Unit.

Cummings, C., Dyson, A., Muijs, D., Papps, I., Pearson, D., Ruffo, C., Tiplady, L., Todd, L. and Crowther, D. (2007) *Evaluation of the Full Service and Extended Schools Initiative: Final Report*. University of Manchester for DCSF.

Day, C., Sammons, P., Hopkins, D., Leithwood, K., Gul, Q., Penlington, C., Mehta, P. and Kington, A. (2009) *Impact of Leadership on Pupil Outcomes*. Final Report to the DCSF.

Department for Children, Schools and Families (DCSF) (2007a) *The Children's Plan: Building Brighter Futures*. Norwich: The Stationery Office.

Department for Children, Schools and Families (DCSF) (2007b) *Extended Schools, Building on Experience*. London: The Stationery Office.

Department for Children, Schools and Families (DCSF) (2008a) *National Challenge: a Toolkit for Schools and Local Authorities*. Nottingham: DCSF Publications.

Department for Children, Schools and Families (DCSF) (2008b) *Vision for London 2008–2011: Education on the Way to World Class*. Nottingham: DCSF Publications.

Department for Education and Employment (DfEE) (1999) *Schools Plus: Building Learning Communities*. Improving the Educational Chances of Children and Young People from Disadvantaged Areas: A Report from the Schools Plus Policy Action Team 11. London: DfEE.

Department for Education and Skills (DfES) (2002a) *The Education Act 2002*. Nottinghamshire: DfES Publications.

Department for Education and Skills (DfES) (2002b) *Investment for Reform*. Nottingham: DfES Publications.

Department for Education and Skills (DFES) (2002c) *Transforming London's Secondary Schools*. London: The Stationery Office.

Department for Education and Skills (DfES) (2003) *A New Specialist System: Transforming Secondary Education*. Nottingham: DfES Publications.

Department for Education and Skills (DfES) (2004) *Guidance on the School Governance (Federations) (England)*. London: The Stationery Office.

Department for Education and Skills (DfES) (2005a) *Higher Standards, Better Schools For All*. Nottingham: DfES Publications.

Department for Education and Skills (DfES) (2005b) *Education Improvement Partnerships: Local Collaboration for School Improvement and Better Service Delivery*. Nottinghamshire: DfES Publications.

Dunford, J. (2006) Show us the money to extend schools, *Times Education Supplement*, 14 July.

Dunford, J. (2005) Watering the plants: leading schools and improving the system. Address to the National Conference of the Specialist Schools and Academies Trust Birmingham, 25 November.

Dunkley, D., Onyett, G. and Shand, R. (2005) *Solihull Excellence Cluster: Full Service Extended Schools Project*. Solihull Metropolitan Borough Council.

Ebbutt, D. (1985) Educational action research: some general concerns and specific quibbles, in R. Burgess (ed.) *Issues in Educational Research: Qualitative Methods*. London: The Falmer Press.

Elmore, R. (2004) *School Reform from the Inside Out: Policy, Practice, and Performance*. Cambridge, MA: Harvard Educational Press.

Feinstein, L., Hearn, B. and Renton, Z. (2007) *Reducing Inequalities: Realising the Talents of All*. London: National Children's Bureau.

Fielding, M., Bragg, S., Craig, J., Cunningham, I., Eraut, M., Gillinson, S., Horne, M., Robinson, C. and Thorp, J. (2005) *Factors Influencing the Transfer of Good Practice*. Nottinghamshire: DfES publications.

Fullan, M. (2004a) *Systems Thinkers in Action: Moving Beyond the Standards Plateau*. Nottingham: Innovation Unit.

Fullan, M. (2004b) *Leadership & Sustainability: System Thinkers in Action*. London: Sage.

Gladwell, M. (2002) *The Tipping Point: How Little Things Can Make a Big Difference*. London: Little Brown.

Glatter, R. (1995) Partnership in the market model: is it dying?, in A. Macbeth, D. McCreath and J. Aitchison (eds) *Collaborate or Compete? Educational Partnerships in a Market Economy*. London: The Falmer Press.

Glatter, R. (2003) Collaboration, collaboration, collaboration: the origins and implications of a policy, *Management in Education*, 17: 16–20.

Glatter, R. and Harvey, J. (2006) *New Models of Headship Varieties of Shared Headship: A Preliminary Exploration*. Nottingham: NCSL.

Gray, J., Hopkins, D., Reynolds, D., Wilcox, B., Farrell, S. and Jesson, D. (1999) *Improving Schools: Performance and Potential*. Buckingham: Open University Press.

Gronn, P. (2003) *The New Work of Education Leaders*. London: Paul Chapman Publishing.

Hannon, V. (2007) New leadership for the collaborative state, in S. Parker and N. Gallagher (eds) *The Collaborative State: How Working Together can Transform Public Services*. London: DEMOS.

Hargreaves, A. and Fink, D. (2006) *Sustainable Leadership*. San Francisco, CA: Jossey-Bass.

Hargreaves, D. (2001) A capital theory of school effectiveness and improvement, *British Educational Research Journal*, 27(4): 487–503.

Hargreaves, D. (2003) *Education Epidemic: Transforming Secondary Schools through Innovation Networks*. London: DEMOS.

Hargreaves, D. (2007) The true meaning of system leadership. Presentation at the NCSL, June.

Harris, A., Brown, D. and Abbott, I. (2006a) Executive leadership: another lever in the system? *School Leadership and Management*, 24(4): 397–409.

Harris, A., Chapman, C., Muijs, D., Russ, J. and Stoll, L. (2006b) Improving schools in challenging contexts: exploring the possible, *School Effectiveness and School Improvement*, 17(4): 409–24.

Hatcher, R. (2008) System leadership, networks and the question of power, *Management in Education*, 22(2): 24–30.

Hawker, D. (2006) Joined-up working: the development of children's services, in G. Pugh and B. Duffy (eds) *Contemporary Issues in the Early Years*. London: SAGE.

Heifetz, R. (1994) *Leadership Without Easy Answers*. Harvard: Belknap Press.

Higham, R. and Hopkins, D. (2007) System leadership for educational renewal in England: the case of Federations and executive heads, *Australian Journal of Education*, 51(3): 299–314.

Higham, R., Hopkins, D. and Ahtaridou, E. (2007) *Improving School Leadership: Country Background Report for England*. Paris: OECD. www.oecd.org/dataoecd/33/45/39279379.pdf (accessed 15 Feb. 2008).

Hill, R. (2006) *Leadership that Lasts: Sustainable School Leadership in the 21st Century*. London: ASCL.

Hill, R. and Matthews, P. (2008) *Schools Leading Schools: The Power and Potential of National Leaders of Education*. Nottingham: NCSL.

HM Treasury (2003) *Every Child Matters*. London: The Stationery Office.

Hopkins, D. (2007a) *Every School a Great School*. Buckingham: Open University Press.

Hopkins, D. (2007b) Working document for the Impact of Leadership on Pupil Outcomes, research project funded by the DCSF (mimeo).

Hopkins, D. (2007c) *Transformation and Innovation: System Leaders in the Global Age*. London: Specialist Schools and Academies Trust.

Hopkins, D. (2008) *A Teacher's Guide to Classroom Research*, 4th edn. Maidenhead: Open University Press.

Hopkins, D. and Higham, R. (2007) System leadership: mapping the landscape, *School Leadership and Management*, 27(2): 147–66.

Hoyle, E. and Wallace, M. (2005) *Educational Leadership: Ambiguity; Professionals and Managerialism*. London: Sage.

Hoyle, E. and Wallace, M. (2007) Educational reform: an ironic perspective, *Educational Management Administration and Leadership*, 35(1): 9–25.

Huxham, C. and Vangen, S. (2005) *Managing to Collaborate: The Theory and Practice of Collaborative Advantage*. London: Routledge.

Jessop, B. (2002) *The Future of the Capitalist State*. Cambridge: Polity.

Katz, D. and Kahn, R. (1966) *The Social Psychology of Organizations*. New York: Wiley.

Kemmis, S. and McTaggart, R. (1988) *The Action Research Planner*, 3rd edn. Geelong: Deakin University.

Knight, J. (2007) Narrowing the gap in life chances. Address at The Fabian Society South-West Conference, Bournemouth, 10 March.

Kofman, F. and Senge, P. (1995) Communities of commitment: the heart of learning organizations, in S. Chawla and J. Renesch (eds) *Learning Organizations: Developing Cultures for Tomorrow's Workplace*. Oregon: Productivity Press.

Kogan, M. (1994) The autonomy of the school, in S. Ranson and J. Tomlinson (eds) *School Co-operation: New Forms of Local Governance*. Harlow: Longman.

Lamb, S. (2007) School reform and inequality in urban Australia: a case of residualising the poor, in R. Teese, S. Lamb, M. Duru-Bellat and S. Helme (eds) *International Studies in Educational Inequality, Theory and Policy Inequality*. Netherlands: Springer.

Leithwood, K., Day, C., Sammons, P., Harris, A. and Hopkins, D. (2006) *Seven Strong Claims about Successful School Leadership*. London: DfES.

Leithwood, K., Jantzi, D. and Steinbach, S. (1999) *Changing Leadership for Changing Times*. Buckingham: Open University Press.

Leithwood, K. and Levin, B. (2005) *Assessing Leadership Effects on Pupil Learning: Part 2 Methodological Issues*. Paper prepared for Department for Education and Skills, UK, March.

Leithwood, K., Louis, K., Anderson, S. and Wahlstrom, K. (2004) *How Leadership Influences Student Learning*. New York: The Wallace Foundation.

Leithwood, K. and Riehl, C. (2003) *What we Know about Successful School Leadership*. Nottingham: NCSL.

Leithwood, K. and Riehl, C. (2005) What we know about successful school leadership, in W. Firestone and C. Riehl (eds) *A new Agenda: Directions for Research on Educational Leadership*. New York: Teachers College Press.

Levačić, R. and Woods, P. (1994) New forms of financial co-operations, in S. Ranson, and J. Tomlinson (eds) *School Co-operation: New Forms of Local Governance*. Harlow: Longman.

Levin, B. (2006) Schools in challenging circumstances: a reflection on what we know and what we need to know, *School Effectiveness and School Improvement*, 17(4): 399–407.

Lindsay, G., Muijs, D., Harris, A., Chapman, C., Arweck, E. and Goodall, J. (2007) *School Federations Pilot Study 2003–2007*. London: DCSF.

Lupton, R. (2005) Social justice and school improvement: improving the quality of school in the poorest neighbourhoods, *British Educational Research Journal*, 31(5): 589–604.

Matthews, P. (2006a) *Aspects of System Leadership: Community Leadership*. Report for the NCSL. London: Institute of Education.

Matthews, P. (2006b) *Procedures used for the Selection of the First National Leaders of Education: Evaluation of the Recruitment and Selection Processes*. Report for the NCSL. London: Institute of Education.

Matthews, P. (2007) *Attributes of the First National Leaders of Education in England: What Do They Bring to the Role?* Nottingham: NCSL.

Matthews, P. (2008) *Emerging Patterns: Aspects of the NLE/NSS Initiative after 18 Months*. Nottingham: NCSL.

Matthews, P. and Sammons, P. (2004) *Improvement through Inspection: An Evaluation of the Impact of Ofsted's Work*. London: Ofsted.

Matthews, P. and Sammons, P. (2005) Survival of the weakest: the differential improvement of schools causing concern in England, *London Review of Education*, 3(2): 159–76.

Matthews, P., Sammons, P., Gu, Q., Day, C. and Smith, P. (2006) *Supporting Leadership and Securing Quality: An Evaluation of the Impact of Aspects of the London Leadership Strategy*. Nottingham: NCSL.

McKernan, J. (1996) *Curriculum Action Research*, 2nd edn. London: Kogan Page.

Miliband, D. (2003) *School Leadership: The Productivity Challenge*, address at the National College for School Leadership, 22 October.

Miliband, D. (2004) *A New Relationship with Schools*, address at the North of England Conference, Belfast, 8 January.

Morris, H. (1924) *The Village College: Being a Memorandum on the Provision of Educational and Social Facilities for the Countryside, with Special Reference to Cambridgeshire*. Cambridge: Cambridge University Press.

Mortimore, P. (1998) *The Road to Improvement: Reflections on School Effectiveness*. Abingdon: Swets and Zeitlinger.

Munby, S. (2006) Letter to schools from the Chief Executive of the National College for School Leadership. Nottingham: NCSL.

National Audit Office (2006) *Improving Poorly Performing Schools in England*. http://www.nao.org.uk/pn/05-06/0506679_full.htm (accessed 4 May 2007).

National College for School Leadership (NCSL) (2005a) *Secondary or Special School Executive Heads: A Study of Heads who are Leading Two or More Secondary or Special Schools*. Nottingham: NCSL.

National College for School Leadership (NCSL) (2005b) *Leadership in Complex Schools: Advice to the Secretary of State*. Nottingham: NCSL.

National College for School Leadership (NCSL) (2006) *School Leaders Leading the System: NCSL's Leadership Network in Conference*. Nottingham: NCSL.

National College for School Leadership (NCSL) (2008) *Asking More of National Leaders of Education*. Policy paper for discussion, NCSL.

Office for Standards in Education (Ofsted) (2003) *Leadership and Management: What Inspection Tells Us*. HMI 1646. London: Ofsted.

Office for Standards in Education (Ofsted) (2004) *Local Education Authority Inspection Report: Brighton and Hove*. London: Ofsted.

Office for Standards in Education (Ofsted) (2006a) *Annual Report: The Annual Report of Her Majesty's Chief Inspector of Schools 2005/06*. London: Ofsted.

Office for Standards in Education (Ofsted) (2006b) *Improvements in London's Schools, 2000–2006*. London: Ofsted.

Office for Standards in Education (Ofsted) (2007) *Annual Performance Assessment of Services for Children and Young People in Brighton and Hove City Council*. London: Ofsted.

O'Leary, D. and Craig, J. (2007) *System Leadership: Lessons from the Literature*. Nottingham: NCSL.

Osbourne, S. (2000) *Public-Private Partnerships*. London: Routledge.

Pont, B., Nusche, D. and Hopkins, D. (2008) *Improving School Leadership – Case Studies on System Leadership*. Paris: OECD.

Potter, D. (2005) *Replicating Effective School Practice as a Tool to Improve the Weakest Schools*. Research Report for the Academies Division, Department for Education and Skills.

Purkey, S. and Smith, M. (1983) Effective schools: a review, *The Elementary School Journal*, 83: 427–62.

Ranson, S. (1994) Local democracy in the learning society, in S. Ranson and J. Tomlinson (eds) *School Co-operation: New Forms of Local Governance*. Harlow: Longman.

Reynolds, D. (2004) *Leading Edge Partnership Programme: An Overview of the Interim Findings – A Qualitative Study*. www.standards.dfes.gov.uk/leadingedge/word/ QualitativeEvaluation.doc?version=1 (accessed 15 Feb. 2008).

Reynolds, D., Hopkins, D., Potter, D. and Chapman, C. (2001) *School Improvement for Schools Facing Challenging Circumstances: A Review of Research and Practice*. Nottinghamshire: DfES Publications.

Rogers, M. (2008) *National Challenge*. Children's Services Network Policy Briefing Number 1896/08C. London: CSN.

Rudd, P., Lines, A., Schagen, S., Simth, R. and Reakes, A. (2004) *Partnership Approaches to Sharing Best Practice*. Slough: NFER.

Rudd, P., Rickinson, M., Blenkinsop, S., McMeeking, S., Taylor, M. and Phillips, N. (2002) *Long-term External Evaluation of the Beacon Schools Initiative 2001–2002*. Slough: NFER.

Rutter, M., Maughan, B., Mortimore, P. and Ouston, J. (1979) *Fifteen Thousand Hours*. London: Paul.

Sammons, P., Hillman, J. and Mortimore, P. (1995) *Key Characteristics of Effective Schools: A Review of School Effectiveness Research*. London: Ofsted.

Sammons, P., Power, S., Elliot, K., Robertson, P., Campbell, C. and Whitty, G. (2003) *New Community Schools in Scotland, Final Report: National Evaluation of the Pilot Phase*. London: Institute of Education.

Senge, P. (1990) *The Fifth Discipline*. New York: DoubleDay.

Smithers, A. and Robinson, P. (2007) *School Headship. Present and Future*. www.nut.org.uk/resources/pdf/Headsfin.pdf (accessed 15 Feb. 2007).

Spender, B. (2006) Linking up for success, *Curriculum Briefing*, 4(2): 28–31.

Stevenson, H. (2007) Improvement through collaboration and competition – can the government have it both ways?, *Management in Education*, 21(1): 29–33.

Stoll, L. (2001) *Enhancing Internal Capacity: Leadership for Learning*. https:// forms.ncsl.org.uk/media/604/DF/enhancing-internal-capacity.pdf (accessed 20 May 2008).

Taylor, C., Gorard, S. and Fitz, J. (2000) *Size Matters: Does School Choice Lead to 'Spirals of Decline'?*, Cardiff University School of Social Sciences Working Paper 36. www.cardiff.ac.uk/socsi/markets/Papers/WP36.pdf (accessed 4 May 2007).

Thrupp, M. (1999) *Schools Making a Difference: Let's be Realistic!* Buckingham: Open University Press.

Vangen, S. and Huxham, C. (2003) Enacting leadership for collaborative advantage: dilemmas of ideology and pragmatism in the activities of partnership managers, *British Journal of Management*, 14: 61–76.

Whitty, G. (1997) Social theory and education policy: the legacy of Karl Mannheim, *British Journal of Sociology of Education*, 18(2): 149–63.

Whitty, G. (2001) Education, social class and social exclusion, *Journal of Education Policy*, 16(4): 287–95.

Index

academies
  management 48
  state schools sponsoring 48
accountability 93
  attempts to streamline 129
  internal 50
  lateral 67–8
  pressures of external on schools 9
action research
  by teachers 63–4
adaptive leadership 25
admissions policies 9
adult education 78
adult institutes 78
Advanced Skills Teachers 12
annual performance assessments
  systems leadership and 83
appointments
  schools 38
area-wide leadership
  NLEs 120
arts
  extended schools and 74
assessment
  learning 57
Association of School and College Leaders
    in England 18
attainment
  ethnic minority groups 38
  student 34, 56
attitudes to learning
  component of effective school 32
Audit Commission 82

Barstable School
  cooperation with Chalverdon School
    91–5
Beacon schools 46
Beacon-partner models
  types of 68–9
behaviour
  component of effective school 32
  implementing systems for 44–5

best practice 19, 39
  ICT 100
  sharing 42
booster classes 43
boys
  underachievement among 53
Brighton and Hove Children and Young
    People's Trust 82
British Cohort study 33
budget deficits 38, 95

Callaghan, James [1912–2005] 13
Cambridgeshire County Council 77
capacity
  building 66
  conception of 65
catch-up
  virtual learning environments for 57
Challney Boys School and Community
    College 77
Chalverdon School
  cooperation with Barstable School 91–5
change agents
  NLEs as 124–7, 142
  school leaders as 25
  SIPs as 142
child and family welfare 24
childcare
  extended schools and 74
  schools providing 75
Children Act (2004) 72, 82, 135
Children, Families and Schools
    Directorate 82
Children and Young People's Plan 84
Children and Young People's Trusts 78
Children's Centres 78, 83
Children's Plans 12, 24
citizen empowerment 143
clarity
  whole-school systems 49
co-construction 61
co-production 138
coaching 111

Coleshill Heath Primary School 73–5, 81
collaboration
 knowledge transfer and 51, 60–4
 Leading Edge Partnership programme
  54–6
 removing barriers to 141
 schools 2–3, 21, 44–7, 138
  benefits of 5
  factors supporting 6
  obstacles to 6
  recent history 3–7
  resolving tensions between
   competition and 7
collaborative innovation 63
 diagrammatic representation 62
command and control policies 4
community colleges 77
community resources
 extended schools 79–80
community schools
 original concept of 78
community-focused schools
 characteristics of 81
competition
 among schools 92, 129
 schools
  resolving tensions between
   collaboration and 7
conferences
 school staff 61
Connexions service 82
Conservative Party 9
 education policies 1, 3
consultant heads 53
consultant leaders 44, 111, 134
 change agents 124–7
 influence of 110
 NLEs 121–2
contextually valued-added (CVA) 36,
 54
continuing professional development *see*
 professional development
continuity 49
 whole-school systems 49
curriculum 57–8 *see also* National
 Curriculum
 component of effective school 32
curriculum pathways 56

delegated budgets
 schools 1

Department for Children, Schools and
 Families (DCSF) 22, 58
 establishment of 82
Department for Education and Skills
 (DfES) 18, 21
deployment
 NLEs 119–24
deprivation funding 53
design
 Leading Edge Partnership programme
  68–70
direction setting
 partner schools 99
disaffection 58
distributed leadership 66
drama
 NSS contribution to 109
Dunford, John 18

Early Excellence Centres 78
education
 global networks 144
 international developments 144
 local management 13
 productivity in 11
 professionalism 3, 8–11
 purpose of 1
 removing barriers to 73–5
 system transformation 138–40
Education Act (2002) 24
Education Epidemic 137
education policies
 Conservative Party 1, 3
 Labour Party 3–4, 93–4, 107
Education Reform Act (1988) 92,
 128
education system
 post-1940s 1
Educational Improvement Partnerships
 24, 105
Educational Improvement Trusts 105
educational policy
 system leadership and 140–2
 United States 125–6
educational reform 26
 schools leading 133
 sustainable 19, 27
 system leadership and 142–5
effective schools
 components of 32–3
Elmore, R. 104

English
  NSS contribution to 109
  SATs 123
entrepreneurship
  extended schools and 86
ethnic minority groups 53
  attainment 38
ethos
  Leading Edge Partnership programme
    68–70
evening classes 78
Every Child Matters (ECM) 11
  effect on schools 72–3
  extended schools and 75–6, 78
  leaders working in context of 24
  local authority changes relating to 82–5
  standards and 89
  system leadership in context of 72–90
Every School a Great School 9
examination results 34, 36–7, 53, 92, 101–
    4, 109
  improvement in 113
  publication of 128
Excellence in Cities programme 4, 129
*Excellence and Fairness: Achieving World
    Class Public Services* 143
executive heads 24, 101–3, 120
  NLEs 121
executive leadership
  federated schools 91–106
expectations 49
experimental implementation 63
extended leadership group 66
extended schools 73–82
  activities 74
  aims and objectives of 75
  community resources for 79–80
  ECM and 75–6
  entrepreneurship and 86
  leadership
    time in post 87–8
  NCSL and 76, 90
  proliferation of under London
    Challenge 114
  resource management 87
  strategic development 86
  succession planning 88
  sustainability 88–9
  system leadership 75–7, 85–9
  team building 88
  vision and purpose 85–6

extension activities
  gifted and talented 58
extra-curricular provision 46

facilitating 111
failing schools 14, 35–7, 41–2, 45, 47–9,
    73–5, 94, 104, 108–12
  changing institutional culture at 43
  evidence and progress and impact 112–4
  involvement of local community 44
  removed from special measures 45
falling rolls 47
federations/co-federations
  benefits of 101–4
  challenges for 104–6
  executive leadership and 91–106
  knowledge transfer 100–1
  lead schools 96–7, 100
  leadership models 97–8
  NCSL and 102
  outcomes 101–4
  partner schools 95–100
  schools 24
  systems management 95–101
Fielding, Michael 137
free school meals 34
Freire, Paulo [1921–97] 146
full-service extended schools 78
  emergence of 76
  management of 77
  school performance and 77
Fullan, Michael 19

GCSE 34, 36, 53, 92, 101–4, 122
  targets for 14
gifted and talented
  extension activities 58
  provision for 46, 58
  virtual learning environments for 57
girls
  education of and Islam 38
Gladwell, Malcolm 136
good practice 5
governments
  role of 143
grant maintained status 38, 92

'hard' federations 95–6
Hargreaves, David 132, 137
headship
  national standards for 27

headteachers
  as ad-hoc consultants to neighbouring
    schools 44–5
  appointment 35–6
  connecting effectiveness of with pupil
    outcomes 132
  increased autonomy of 128
  interaction with each other 12
  providing support to other schools 47
  supporting 44
health and social care
  extended schools and 74
high deprivation schools
  free school meals in 34
Higher Standards, Better Schools for All
  main provisions of 11–2
home-school liaison officer 80
Hospital Trusts 82

'immersion' teaching and learning
    programme 109
Impact of Leadership on Pupil Outcomes
    project 130–1
Impington Village College 77
implementation
  experimental 63
improvement *see* school improvement
in-service training 42
independence
  schools 142
inductive development 62
inequalities 8
iNet 144
information
  analysis of 63
  sharing and exchange 44
information and communication
    technology (ICT) 41
  best practice in 100
  developments in use of 60
  early introduction of 42
  extended schools and 74
  NSS contribution to 109
  support for teaching 57
initiatives
  constant stream of relating to schools
    9
innovation
  emergence of 41
  leadership of 51–71
  transfer of 136–8

innovation and improvement
  partnerships 24, 51–71
  building capacity for 64–5
  leadership of 64–70
innovation trios 61
Innovation Unit 52
inspections
  Ofsted 42
institutional culture
  changing 43
institutional and leadership capabilities
  hypotheses for 48–50
intellectual capital 65
interim headteachers 125
internal accountability
  component of effective school 33
interviews
  semi-structured 35
Investment for Reform 108
Islam
  girls' education and 38

joint planning
  strategies 63
joint practice development 100

Key Stage 3 Strategy 42
Knight, Jim 93
knowledge transfer
  collaborative working and 51,
    60–4
  federations/co-federations 100–1
  obstacles to 60–1

Labour Party 9
  education policies 3–4, 93–4, 107
lateral accountability 67–8
lateral working 4
lead schools
  federations/co-federations 96–7, 100
'leadership by adjective' literature 26
leadership
  component of effective school 32
  innovation and improvement
    partnerships 64–70
  of learning 66
  management and 46
  new models of 65–7
  time in post
    extended schools 87–8
Leadership Incentive Grant 4, 53, 129

leadership models
  federations/co-federations 97–8
leadership roles
  development of 40
leadership support 56
'leading edge'
  concept of 52
Leading Edge Partnership programme 12,
  22, 51–71, 116, 138
  aims and objectives 52
  annual conference (2007) 54
  building capacity 64–5
  collaborative advantages 54–6
  deployment of funds 69–70
  ethos and design 68–70
  funding for participation 52
  government expectations of 68
  lateral accountability 67–8
  new leadership models 65–7
  Oldham 53–4
  schools 46, 137
  system leadership in 69–71
learner-centred systems 135
learning
  assessment 57
  development of new strategies 57
  improving quality of 49
  positive attitudes to 43
learning community
  component of effective school 32
learning support 80
'learning walks' 61
lifelong learning 24
  extended schools and 74
literacy
  development of skills 49
literacy support 41
local authorities
  changes to 82–5
local authority data groups 53
local authority directors 12
local education authorities (LEAs) 4,
  45
Local Leaders of Education 125
local management of schools (LMS) 13,
  128
local partnerships
  schools 2, 4
local strategic leadership 5
London Challenge 107–14, 117, 120, 126
  aims and objectives 113–4

  comparative performance between
    London and national students 114
  consultant leaders 108
  key partners in 108
  proliferation of extended schools and
    114
London Leadership Strategy (LLS) 108–9,
  117, 119
looked after children 84
low attaining schools 20, 24
low deprivation schools
  free school meals in 34
low expectations
  challenging 56–7

management
  academies 48
Management of Quality Teaching and
  Learning Group 67
market forces
  schools 1, 4, 92
mathematics
  extension activities 58
  improvement strategies for 47
  SATs 123
media studies
  NSS contribution to 109
mentor heads 22
mentoring 47, 56, 111
Miliband, David Wright 11
Morris, Estelle 107
Morris, Henry [1889–1962] 77
motivation 64
  students 56, 58
mutuality of process 61

narrative for improvement 37–9
National Challenge 12, 14, 21, 108
National College for School Leadership
  (NCSL) 20, 88, 123, 129
  federations/co-federations and 76, 90,
    102
National Curriculum 9
  introduction of 4
National Foundation for Educational
  Research 68
National Health Service (NHS) 82
National Leaders of Education (NLEs) 12,
  22, 24–5, 47, 105, 107–8
  appointment of 115
  area-wide leadership 120

change agents 124–7, 142
characteristics of 116–8
consultant leaders 121–2
deployment of 119–24
emergence of 135
executive heads 121
impact of 122–4
role of 115–8
support consultants 119–20
system director 119–20
National Literacy Strategy 42
National Professional Qualification for
  Headship (NPQH) 88
National Strategies 39
development of 4
National Support Schools (NSSs) 47, 105,
  107, 109, 116–7, 119
emergence of 135
national tests 4
networking
increased importance of 129
schools 2–3
networks
SSAT 45
for transferred innovation 137
New Relationship with Schools 11, 129
notice to improve 20, 109
numeracy
development of skills 49

observed teaching
Ofsted 42
Ofsted 34–5, 38, 45, 47, 53, 75, 82, 109,
  112
inspections 42
observed teaching 42
Oldham
Leading Edge Partnerships in 53–4
Organization for Economic Co-operation
  and Development (OECD) 128, 144–5
organizational capital 65
organizational development
partner schools 100
organizational redesign 132
outcomes
federations/co-federations 101–4
outreach 135
Outwood Grange School 132
overstaffing 95

parental involvement 38

virtual learning environments for
  57
parenting support
extended schools and 74
Parents' Association 80
Parents' Centre 80
partner schools 53
federations/co-federations 95–100
improvement process in 99–100
partnerships 51–71
component of effective school 33
peer observation and feedback 63
peer training 42
performance tables 9
personalized learning 70
diagrammatic approach to 59
Leading Edge Partnership programme
  and 57–60
Pittsburgh Institute 61
planning meetings 42
informal 61
Police Authority 82
preventive services 83
Primary Care Trusts 82
Primary National Strategy [formerly
  National Literacy and National
  Numeracy Strategies] 134
Primary Networks 129
primary schools
improving standards 107
Primary Strategy Consultant leaders
  12
productivity
education 11
professional action
culture of 43
professional development 5, 22, 41–2,
  141
Leading Edge Partnership programme
  55
professional engagement 4, 62
professional support
Leading Edge Partnership programme
  55
professionalism 3, 8–11, 133
school leadership 129
progress
failing schools 112–4
public sector professionals 13
public services
reform of 142–3

recruitment
  school staff 33
redundancy 38
regeneration 92
research 61
resource management
  component of effective school 33
  extended schools 87
resources 5
retention
  school staff 33
revision
  virtual learning environments for 57
River Leen school 47
Roach, Alan 91, 94

SATs
  English 123
  Mathematics 123
Saturday opening
  schools 43
Sawston Village College 77
school development
  Leading Edge Partnership programme
    55
  NLEs 120
  planning 43
school environment 35
school governors 45
  devolving resource allocation to 128
school holidays
  childcare 75
school improvement
  building capacity for 64–5
  key activities for 39–40
  Leading Edge Partnership programme 55
  main stages of 37–44
  narrative for improvement 37–9
  NLEs 120
  partner schools 99–100
  principles for 39
  regular review of 39–40
  relationship with system leadership 31–50
  strategies for 47
  sustained 31–50
  system leaders determining capacity for
    49
School Improvement Partners (SIPs) 11–2,
    22, 25, 134, 141
  as change agents 142
  headteacher as 46–7

school improvement plans 67
school inspections 128
school leaders
  as change agents 25
  declining supply of 20
  working in context of ECM 24
school leadership
  evolving 128–30
  extending 7
  increasing professionalism of 129
  primacy of 130–3
  school transformation and 131
School Leadership for Systemic Improvement
    144
school organization 58
school performance
  full service extended schools and 77
school staff 45
  conferences 61
school systems
  development of 40
school-community dynamic 78–81
schools
  appointments 38
  attempts to streamline accountability
    129
  booster classes 43
  categorization of 139
  change agents for transformation
    107–27
  changing institutional culture at 43
  changing role within community 77–81
  characteristics of community-focused
    81
  collaboration 2–3, 21, 44–7, 138
    benefits of 5
    factors supporting 6
    obstacles to 6
    resolving tensions between
      competition and 7
  competition 92, 129
    resolving tensions between
      collaboration and 7
  components of effective 32–3
  constant stream of initiatives relating to
    9
  coordinating work of social service
    agencies into 26
  delegated budgets 1
  extended 73–80
    activities 74

schools—*cont*
aims and objectives of 75
community resources for 79–80
ECM and 75–6
entrepreneurship and 86
leadership
time in post 87–8
NCSL and 76, 90
resource management 87
strategic development 86
succession planning 88
sustainability 88–9
system leadership 75–7, 85–9
team building 88
vision and purpose 85–6
failing 14, 35–7, 41–2, 45, 47–9, 73–5,
94, 104, 108–12
changing institutional culture at 43
evidence and progress and impact
112–4
involvement of local community 44
removed from special measures 45
federations/co-federations 24
flexibility of 75
historical isolation of 1
independence of 142
Leading Edge Partnership programme 46
leading educational reform 133
local partnerships 2, 4
low attaining 20, 24
market forces 1, 4, 92
networking 2–3
notice to improve 20
partner 53
pressures of external accountability on
9
Saturday opening 43
self-evaluation 67
socioeconomic background 34, 49
in special measures 20
system leadership 1–17
key roles 2–3
underperforming 24
voluntary organizations and 5
whole-school improvement 20
Schools Plus report 75
science
extension activities 58
secondary schools
improving standards 107
transition to 58

semi-structured interviews 35
senior management team (SMT) 35,
39–43, 45–6, 78
Serco Education [formerly Quality
Assurance Associates] 47
Seven Strong Claims about School Leadership
130
social capital 65
social justice 11
social segregation 53
social service agencies
coordinating work of into a school 26
socioeconomic background
schools 34, 49–50
special educational needs (SEN) 46
special measures 20, 47, 92
removal from from 45
Specialist Schools and Academies Trust
(SSAT) 18, 52, 139
Leading Edge programme team 68
networks 45
sports
extended schools and 74
staff development
partner schools 99
staff loss 65
staff recruitment and retention 33
staff review 38
standards 7–8
balance between welfare and 129
ECM and 89
national for headship 27
primary schools 107
secondary schools 107
state schools
number of 1
strategic development
extended schools 86
strategies
joint planning 63
Stringfield, Sam 125–6
student attainment 34, 56
student data
use for assessment 57
student involvement 58
student outcomes
Leading Edge Partnership programme
55
student transition 41
student welfare 4
improving 49

students
  feedback from 63
  motivation 58
  motivation and support 56
  support 58
  tracking systems 53, 56
study support
  extended schools and 74
succession planning
  extended schools 88
Suffolk Council 84
'super heads' 22, 31, 133
support
  students 58
support consultants 109
support staff
  number of 1
Sure Start programme 76, 78
sustainability
  extended schools 88–9
  school improvement 31–50
system coherence 4
system director
  NLEs 119–20
system leaders
  determining capacity for improvement
      49
  key capabilities for 28
  role of 25–9
  school 8
System Leaders in Action 8
system leadership 13–4, 26–7, 66, 133
  annual performance assessment and 83
  categories of 133–4
  challenges for 89–90
  community-focused schools 81
  context of Every Child Matters, in
      72–90
  cynicism over 133
  developing 141–2
  educational policy and 140–2
  educational reform 142–5
  emergence of 1–17, 133–5
  extended schools 75–7, 85–9
  extent of 22
  federations/co-federations 95–101
  key roles in 2–3
  landscape of 21–3
  Leading Edge Partnership programme
      69–71
  levels of 140

system leadership—*cont*
  meaning of 135
  model of practice 29
  as national policy or professional
      movement 19
  prospects for 30, 128–46, 145–6
  relationship with school improvement
      31–50
  taxonomy of roles 18, 23–5
  wider system roles 44–8
system management *see* system leadership
system organization
  forms of 7–8
system partnership
  definition of 135
System Thinkers in Action 19
system thinking 8, 33
system transformation
  education 138–40

target groups 56
  identification of focus of 63
targeting
  student progress 47
targets 3
taxonomy
  proposed for system leadership 18
  system leadership 23–5
teacher development programmes 109
teachers
  number of 1
teaching
  development of new strategies 57
  ICT support for 57
  improving quality of 49
  raising standards of 109
teaching and learning
  component of effective school 32
  managing 132–3
teaching schools 109
teaching skills 39
team building
  extended schools 88
Thatcher, Margaret Hilda 3
theory of action 26
Third Way
  Labour Party's 4
Tipping Point, The 136
tracking systems
  student 53, 56
transferred innovation 136–8

Transforming Middle Leaders Programme
132
transition
secondary school 58

underachievement
boys 53
underperforming schools 24
unexpected events 65
United States
educational policy 125–6
urban regeneration 77–8

'validated' packages
delivery of 60
value-added outcomes 49
virtual learning environments 57
vocational education 100
voluntary organizations
schools and 5

welfare
balance between standards and 129
well-being
children 73–5
Whitty, Geoffrey James 106
whole-school improvement 20
whole-school in-service training 65
whole-school systems
clarity 49
continuity 49
whole-school tracking 47
workforce reform 41

Year 11 students
support for 47
youth service 78

IMPROVING URBAN SCHOOLS
Leadership and Collaboration

Mel Ainscow and Mel West (eds)

The improvement of urban schools is one of the major challenges facing practitioners and policy-makers today. Issues related to poverty create particular difficulties in urban schools, and the emphasis on market-led improvement strategies has tended to add to these challenges. In addition, strategies for 'raising standards', as measured by aggregate test and examination results, can result in marginalisation or exclusion of some groups of learners.

Drawing on research evidence, *Improving Urban Schools* addresses the question of how primary and secondary urban schools can be improved in a more inclusive way. The authors argue that urban schools and their communities have within them expertise that tends to be overlooked, and latent creativity that should be mobilised to move thinking and progress forward. They show that new approaches to leadership, various forms of collaborative school-to-school partnerships, and major changes in national policy development are needed to make use of this untapped energy.

The book includes vivid accounts of these activities to shed light on what really happens in urban schools, and presents practical strategies for school leaders and practitioners who want to make a difference in urban schools.

Contributors: *Mel Ainscow, Alan Dyson, Samantha Fox, Helen Gunter, Andy Howes, Andrew Morley, Maria Nicolaidou, Jacqui Stanford, Dave Tweddle, Mel West.*

Contents: *Notes on contributors - Series preface - Editors preface - Preface - The challenge of urban school improvement - The experience of failure in urban primary schools - The development of leadership capacity in a school facing challenging circumstances - Leading developments in practice: Barriers and possibilities - Achieving sustainable improvements in urban schools - Confounding stereotypes: Risk, resilience and achievement in urban schools - Moving practice forward at the district level - Supporting schools in difficult circumstances: The role of school to school cooperation - Moving leadership practice in schools forward - Collaboration with a city-wide purpose: Making paths for sustainable educational improvement - Beyond the school gates: Context, disadvantage and 'urban schools' - Drawing out the lessons: Leadership and collaboration - References - Index.*

2006 180pp
978-0-335-21911-7 (Paperback) 978-0-335-21912-4 (Hardback)

EVERY SCHOOL A GREAT SCHOOL
Realising the Potential of System Leadership

David Hopkins

'Every school a great school' is not just a slogan, but an aspiration for the next stage of education reform, in which each student has the opportunity to reach their full potential.

The book argues that, for 'every school a great school' to become a reality, requires a move from individual school improvement efforts and short term objectives to a sustainable system-wide response that seeks to re-establish a balance between national prescription and schools leading reform.

Achieving this goal requires strategies that not only continue to raise standards, but also build capacity within the system. David Hopkins identifies four key educational 'drivers' that, if pursued, have the potential to deliver 'every school a great school':

- Personalised learning
- Professionalised teaching
- Networking and innovation
- Intelligent accountability

The author believes that it is the responsibility of system leaders to mould the four drivers to fit individual school contexts. It is this leadership that enables systemic reform to be generic in terms of overall strategy and specific in adapting to individual and particular situations.

Every School a Great School is inspirational reading for head teachers, senior leaders and managers, researchers, lecturers and those with a passionate interest in improving education for all.

Contents: *Introduction - PART 1 The context of system reform - Every school a great school - From large-scale change to system-wide reform - PART 2 The four drivers of system reform - Personalized learning - Professionalized teaching - Intelligent accountability - Networking and innovation - PART 3 Realizing the system leadership dividend - The power of system leadership - Moving system leadership to scale - Bibliography - Index.*

March 2007 216pp
ISBN-13: 978 0 335 22099 1 (ISBN-10: 0 335 22099 1) Paperback
ISBN-13: 978 0 335 22100 4 (ISBN-10: 0 335 22100 9) Hardback

PROFESSIONAL LEARNING COMMUNITIES
Divergence, Depth and Dilemmas

Louise Stoll and Karen Seashore Louis (eds)

"All who are interested and concerned about educational reform and the improvement of schools will find this book a must read. It stimulates, it challenges, and it informs, such that the reader is most surely enriched by its plenitude."

Dr Shirley Hord, Scholar Emerita

"At last we have a book of international cases to add to the literature on networks! Policymakers and practitioners alike will find the reasons why networks are fast becoming the reform organizations of choice. The book elevates network understanding to a new level."
Ann Lieberman, Senior Scholar at the Carnegie Foundation for the Advancement of Teaching

- What is a Professional Learning Community?
- What are the key challenges facing these communities and how might they be resolved?
- Is it time to extend our thinking about Professional Learning Communities?

There is great interest internationally in the potential of professional learning communities for enhancing educational reform efforts and sustaining improvement. This international collection expands perceptions and understanding of professional learning communities within and beyond schools, as well as highlighting frequently neglected complexities and challenges.

Drawing on research, each chapter offers a deeper understanding of topics such as distributed leadership, dialogue, organizational memory, trust, self-assessment and inquiry, and purpose linked to learning. Three of the most challenging dilemmas facing professional learning communities are explored – developing professional learning communities in secondary schools, building social capital, and sustaining professional learning communities. The authors provide pointers on why these challenges exist, offering rays of hope for ways forward.

This book is a must-read for anyone interested in building capacity for sustainable learning and the ability to harness your community as a resource for change.

Contents: List of figures and tables - List of contributors - Series editors' preface - Acknowledgements - Professional learning communities: Elaborating new approaches - Part 1: Divergence - The involvement of support staff in professional learning communities - Extending the learning community: A broader perspective embedded in policy - From professional learning community to networked learning community - Beyond borders: Can international networks deepen professional learning community? - Part 2: Depth - 'Normalizing' problems of practice: Converting routine conversation into a resource for learning in professional communities - How leaders use artifacts to structure professional community in schools - Developing collective understanding over time: Reflections on building professional community - Using assessment tools as frames for dialogue to create and sustain professional learning communities - Transforming practice from within: The power of the professional learning community - Part 3: Dilemmas - Building professional learning communities in high schools: Challenges and promising practices - Building social capital in professional learning communities: Importance, challenges and a way forward - Sustainable professional learning communities - Part 4: Afterword - Professional learning communities: A reflection - Index.

2007 232pp
978-0-335-22030-4 (Paperback) 978-0-335-22031-1 (Hardback)